Biography

DAVID SEDARIS

A Life Of Sharp Tongue, Happy Turns, And Lucky Escapes

William Adams

TABLE OF CONTENTS

TABLE OF CONTENTS
    CHAPTER 1
    A BULLET OFF-CENTER
    CHAPTER 2
    FATHER TIME FALLS
    CHAPTER 3
    ECCHYMOSE
    CHAPTER 4
    I'VE GOT YOU (TOO LATE)
    CHAPTER 5
    GOD AND THE NAIL AD
    CHAPTER 6
    HOT DOGS AND HAND SANITIZER
    CHAPTER 7
    HOW DO WE GET TO THE OTHER SIDE?
    CHAPTER 8
    KING OF CLUTTER, PRINCE OF TURTLES
    CHAPTER 9
    HE DIED, NOT PASSED
    CHAPTER 10
    SUMMER TEETH
    CHAPTER 11
    THE SPLINTERS BENEATH MY SKIN
    CHAPTER 12
    FIG ON THE CONCOURSE

CHAPTER 1
A BULLET OFF-CENTER

*I*t was spring, and my sister Lisa and I were driving from the Greensboro, North Carolina, airport to her Winston-Salem home in her toy-sized automobile. I had woken up early to catch my flight from Raleigh, but she was an hour ahead of me. "I like to be at Starbucks right when they open, at five a.m.," she told me. "I was there a few months back and observed a lady with a monkey. I'm not sure what sort it was, but it was small—about the size of a doll—and dressed in a pink frilly outfit. It was really upsetting for me. I wanted to approach this woman and ask, "What do you intend to do with that thing once you've lost interest in it?"'

Lisa, like many other pet owners I know, believes that no one can care for an animal better than she can. "Look at how that guy is dragging his Irish setter on a leash!" " she will say, pointing to what appears to be a man walking his dog. Or, if the dog is not on a leash: "That beagle's about to be hit by a car, and his owner's not doing anything about it." No one's spaniel has the necessary vaccines. Nobody's bird is feeding properly or having its toenails clipped to the appropriate length.

"What made you so certain this woman would lose interest in her monkey? "

Lisa gave me the expression that indicated, "A monkey—of course she's going to lose interest in it."

We came upon a billboard promoting ProShots, a gun range, near there.

"I think we should go to that place and shoot guns," Lisa said me.

So, the next afternoon, we arrived for our three-o'clock appointment. I had expected that a firing range would be outside, but it was actually located in a strip mall, adjacent to a tractor-supply business. Inside, there were glass display cases full of weapons and a wall of bags where a woman might conceal a little revolver. This was a niche sector I was unfamiliar with until I got to Lisa's house later that day and looked it up online. There, I discovered websites that sold gun-concealing vests, T-shirts, jackets, and more. One firm offers boxer briefs with a holster in the back, which they call "Compression Concealment Shorts" but I would refer it as gunderpants.

Lisa and I had a good time browsing throughout the store. ROSSI R352—$349.77, according to a tag alongside one of the pistols. If I were in an office supply store, I could have made a pricing estimate, but I have no notion how much a pistol costs. It was like pricing penguins or milking machinery. My shooting experience was restricted to air rifles. Lisa had no experience, so before we went on the firing range, we sat for a forty-minute gun-safety class conducted by Lonnie, a retired Winston-Salem police officer who co-owned the firm and was wearing one of its T-shirts. The man was probably in his early forties, with pale brows and wire-rimmed, practically invisible glasses framed by a baseball cap bearing the Blackwater emblem. He may not be your ideal friend, but you wouldn't mind having him as a neighbor. "I shoveled your driveway while you were asleep," you could see him saying. "I hope you do not mind. "I just wanted to exercise."

There was a classroom in the back of the business, and after seated us side by side at one of the desks, Lonnie took the chair across from us. "The first thing you should understand about firearm safety is that most people are stupid. I don't mean you specifically, but people in general. So, I have a few rules. Number one: Always presume that each weapon is loaded."

Lisa and I leaned back, wincing as he placed two weapons in front of us. The first was a Glock, and the second—the nicer-looking one—was a snub-nosed .38 Special.

"Now, are they loaded? He asked.

"I am going to assume that they are," Lisa replied.

Lonnie replied, "Good girl."

I once discovered a gun while cleaning someone's apartment in New York. It was beneath the bed where the pornography should have been, wrapped in a T-shirt, and it was in my lap before I understood what it was. Then I froze, just like I would have if it was a bomb. I gently nudged it back into position, wondering what the person who owned it looked like, as I had never met him.

I used to believe that males with beards carried guns. Then I understood, after asking around, that men with beards had fathers who owned guns. It was remarkable how accurate this was. I once met an Asian American man with a very sketchy goatee—no more than a dozen eyelash-length hairs on his chin—and when I speculated that his father had bullets but no gun, he gasped, "Oh my God." How did you know? "

This was before beards became popular again and everyone started growing them. Now, I believe that people who wear baseball caps with sunglasses perched on the brims carry guns, especially if the sunglasses' lenses are mirrored or fade from orange to yellow, like a tequila sunrise. I'm not sure about the women.

Lonnie had moved on by this point, and he was showing us how to pick up our firearms. Like most people raised on water pistols and dart-shooting plastic Lugers, we instinctively sought for the triggers, which is a no-no in the Big Book of Safety. "These weapons absolutely cannot fire unless you tug that little piece of metal," Lonnie informed the crowd.

"What if you drop them? They won't go off. "I asked.

"Absolutely not," he replied. "Almost never. So, David, pick up your Glock."

I overcame my fear and followed the instructions.

"Great job! "

When Lisa's turn came, her finger went straight to the trigger.

"Busted," Lonnie informed her. "OK, now, David, I want you to pick up the thirty-eight, and Lisa, you go for the Glock."

We'd just gotten to rule number two—never point your weapon at another person unless you plan to kill or harm them—when Lisa revealed why she was attending the class: "What if someone tries to shoot me? And accidently drops the gun? I'd like to know how to handle it appropriately.

"That is a very good, very smart reason," Lonnie explained. "I can tell you're someone who thinks ahead."

Oh, you had no idea, I thought.

Our safety practice ran a little longer than planned, but we still had ten minutes of shooting time, which was more than enough in retrospect. Lisa standing ramrod straight with a loaded Glock in her hand was as surprising to me as seeing her in front of an orchestra waving a baton. Her first bullet struck the target—a life-sized silhouette of a man—but missed the bull's-eye of his heart by an inch at most.

Where did that come from? I wondered.

"Good girl!" "Lonnie told her. "Now I want you to plant your legs a little farther apart and try again."

Her second shot came even closer.

"Lisa, you're a natural," Lonnie stated. "OK, Mike, now you give it a try."

I looked around, puzzled. "Excuse me?" "

He handed me the .38. "You came here to shoot, right? "

I took the gun, and from then until we left, my name was Mike, which was more than a bit disheartening. Not understanding the "Wait a minute—the David Sedaris?" " I had come to anticipate that meeting someone would be awful enough, but being converted into Mike? I recalled the day a woman approached me in a hotel lobby. "Pardon me," she asked, "but are you here for the Lions Club meeting? "That is the Mike of organizations.

Lonnie did not forget my sister's name; rather, he wore it out. "A good shot, Lisa! Now do it with your left eye closed." "So, Lisa, are you ready to tackle the thirty-eight? "

"Do I have to?" " she asked. The truth was that she—and we—were already bored. As I took my final image, I thought of a couple I know in Odessa, Texas. Tom repairs airplanes, so he and Randy live directly at the airport, in a prefabricated house next to the hangar where he works. One late night, a huge, crazy-looking man who turned out to be an escaped mental patient drove through the high chain-link fence that surrounded their property and hammered on their door. "I know you have my mother in there!" " he yelled. "I know you have her captive, you bastard! "

It was crazy what he was saying, yet there was no stopping him.

Tom and Randy were on the other side of the door, bracing it with their bodies, and when it began to fall off its hinges, Tom sprinted for his revolver.

"Do you have a gun?" " I inquired, astonished, perhaps, since he is gay.

Tom nodded. "I fired at where I thought his knees would be, but he was bent over at the time, so the bullet went into his neck."

It did not kill him, however. Enraged, the freed mental patient returned to the wheel and drove through the large garage-style door of the hangar. Then he exited through the rear wall and onto the tarmac, making a U-turn and driving into Tom and Randy's house.

"Wait," I replied. "This is like a movie where the villain refuses to die."

"I understand! "Agreed Randy, who leads his local arts council. "I'm the pacifist in this relationship; I've never carried a gun in my life, but there I was as this insane man drove passed my chest of drawers, shrieking, 'Kill him! '"

As Tom leveled his rifle again, the man passed out from blood loss, and the police arrived shortly after. By then, the door was hanging by a thread with bullet holes, the hangar had been nearly damaged, and a stolen car lay at the foot of their bed. This, I reasoned, is precisely why people buy firearms. The NRA could have turned their tale into a commercial.

Who do I want to shoot? I asked myself, staring at the figure in front of me and wondering if there was a female counterpart. Of course, it didn't matter who I envisioned killing. My sole hope was that my enemies would laugh themselves to death because the bullet I fired was so far off target.

At the end of our session, Lonnie pulled in our target and inscribed Lisa's name above the bullet hole closest to the heart. He wrote "Mike" over the one that was farthest away before rolling it up and handing it to us as a gift. Later, as I paid, Lonnie mentioned that North Carolina had quite excellent laws. "We're a very gun-friendly state," he informed me.

When I informed him that in England, a guy was sentenced to prison for shooting a burglar who was breaking into his home, Lonnie's jaw fell. It was as if I had told that where I live, you must walk on your hands between the hours of six a.m. It's midday. "That's crazy," he said. Turning to the person next to him, he asked, "Did you hear that? " He went back to me and said, "I'm telling you, Mike, sometimes I don't know what this world is coming to."

There were several bumper stickers in the glass case beneath the counter, one of which read PROSHOTS: PANSIES CONVERTED DAILY.

"That used to be on their billboard until gay people complained," Lisa explained as we headed out the door.

I'm not someone who gets quickly upset. There's a lot I dislike about this planet. There's a lot of stuff that makes me upset, but the only things that really annoy me, that actually offend my sense of decency, are cartoons in which animals wear sunglasses and exclaim "awesome" all the time. That, in my opinion, goes too far. It's not because the animal in question—a rabbit, bear, or whatever—is being insulted, but because it's teaching youngsters to be average. Calling homosexual folks pansies is just "meh," in my opinion.

"What was the deal with the'reason for taking the class'? "I asked Lisa as we walked across the parking lot to her car. "Why do you think your attacker is going to drop his gun? "

She unlocks her door and opens it. "I do not know. Perhaps he'll wear gloves and lose his grip."

As we drove away, I wondered if sad people ever took the safety class and then turned the weapons on themselves once they were on the firing range. "It would be more practical than buying your own Glock or thity-eight, and there'd be no mess," I claimed. "At least not at your home. And, since you don't pay until the end of the session, it won't cost you anything. Except for your life."

Lisa contemplated it. "I always thought that before I committed suicide, I'd first kill Henry." She was referring to her parrot, who could easily live to be seventy. "Don't get me wrong, I adore him to pieces. I really do not want him to be abused after I am gone."

"I thought he went to me after you died," I told him.

Lisa indicated for a turn. "You'd just lose interest in him."

Sandy Hook occurred shortly after we completed our safety class. Two months later, ProShots sent an email with a Valentine message. It was a photograph depicting a heart shape formed out of weaponry. There were pistols and semiautomatic rifles. Even hand grenades. I read that following the shooting, gun purchases increased, with the worry that President Obama would eliminate the Second Amendment. The same thing happened after the shooter opened fire in a Colorado movie theater and the slaughter at South Carolina's Emanuel African Methodist Episcopal Church.

It's so odd to me to desire to own a gun, especially one that might be used in a conflict. I'm not sure why, but shooting doesn't appeal to me. I attempted it once with Lisa and don't feel the desire to do it again. People on YouTube destroy bowling pins and ancient toaster ovens in their backyards, and I just don't understand it. I've never thought of stalking and killing my own food. I'm not concerned that a race war will break out and that I'll need to prepare for it. I'm not worried that an escaped lunatic will burst down my front door in the middle of the night. Things like that do happen, but I'd rather prepare by having a back door. Where I reside today, in the United Kingdom, it is difficult to obtain a rifle and nearly impossible to obtain a pistol. Despite all odds, British people feel free. Is it that they don't realize what they're missing? Or does the freedom they experience come from not being shot to death in a classroom, shopping mall, or movie theater?

Of fact, stabbings in the UK are on the rise, but a knife can only murder a few people at once. Furthermore, there is no movement created around bladed weapons in the same way that there is for firearms. I have yet to see a bumper sticker with a fencing sword and the words COME AND TAKE IT or THINK TWICE, BECAUSE I WON'T. A few days after Sandy Hook, I went online and noticed an ad for the Bushmaster, one of Adam Lanza's weapons. It featured an assault rifle and the phrase CONSIDER YOUR MAN CARD REISSUED.

Every school shooting is unique, but similar. The news footage shows crying youngsters, flowers, and teddy bears in a mound being rained on. There are reports that the community is "healing," and then they move on to the next one. The solution, according to the NRA, is for more people to own weapons. After the deadly shooting in Parkland, Florida, President Trump recommended arming teachers. I called Lisa, who seemed skeptical. "Wait a second," she replied. "Where did you read this?" "

A few years ago, I considered a dinner. My sister joined me for a weekend in Chicago and asked my friend Adam, "Are you familiar with a newspaper called The Onion?" "

"Of course," he replied.

"See? I had no idea what that was. Then I saw an article suggesting that, in order to save money, American schools would eliminate the past tense. After I completed it, I called my husband and told him, 'This is the last straw.' Because I used to teach, and budgets are being cut these days, this sounded entirely possible to me."

"How can you save money by removing the past tense? " Adam inquired.

"I don't know," Lisa replied. "I guess I wasn't thinking clearly."

It's probably best that someone as gullible is no longer in front of a class. Still, I don't blame her for not trusting the armed-teacher story. Who would have imagined that once everything was said and done, this would be the suggested solution? A few days later, the Blue Mountain School District in eastern Pennsylvania placed buckets of river rocks in all of its classrooms, with the intention of encouraging students to stone their would-be murderers.

I believe a few would reach for a rock, but wouldn't the majority freeze or start crying? I know I would.

Then came Santa Fe, Texas, where, to my family's great dismay, the shooter's name was Dimitrios Pagourtzis.

We felt the same way that Korean Americans most certainly did after Virginia Tech.

"Oh no," we said. "He is one of us!" "

Fortunately, the state's lieutenant governor blamed the building's multitude of exits and entrances rather than Greece. "The school that I taught at is now holding active-shooter drills," said Lisa. "That's where the students—and mine were third graders—turn off the lights and hide in dark corners." She was sighing. "I'm just glad I got out when I did."

During the Cuban missile crisis, my sister and I participated in atomic-bomb drills as children. Instead of leading us to shelters twelve stories underground, our teachers instructed us to crouch beneath our desks. What were we thinking as we kneeled there, hands atop our heads? Did we believe that the bombs would only blow off a few ceiling tiles, and that when we returned home, everything would be exactly as we had left it? Our parents, our pets, food, perhaps with a little dust on it?

Children can better understand the concept of being shot. If you have a television in your home, you are familiar with the concept of a gun and what occurs when people are shot. You may not have a strong understanding of death—its permanence, refusal to be negotiated with—but you know it is bad. At the time, Lisa was in second grade and I was in first, and the atomic bomb was simply a concept. So when I saw my sister on the school bus at the end of a drill day—in a dress and patent-leather shoes, her hair just so, looking far more elegant than she ever would as an adult—I wouldn't be relieved, but rather excited, as kids that age are when they're released into the world at the end of the day. Oh to be alive and free.

CHAPTER 2
FATHER TIME FALLS

*M*y father fell in his kitchen the night before his ninety-fifth birthday. My sister Lisa and her husband, Bob, stopped by hours later to put up his new TV and found him on the floor, dazed and in pain. After they helped him up, he fell again, prompting the call for an ambulance. They arrived at the hospital with our sister Gretchen and Amy, who had come in from New York to attend the now-canceled celebration. "It was really weird," she stated when we talked on the phone the next morning. "Dad assumed Lisa was Mom, and when the doctor asked where he was, he said 'Syracuse'—where he went to college. Then he became enraged and remarked, 'You're certainly asking a lot of questions.' As if that's not typical for a doctor. I believe he felt this was just a man he was talking to."

Fortunately, he was lucid again by the next afternoon. The worst part for everyone was watching him so bewildered.

On the night my father fell, I was in Princeton, New Jersey, the fourth of eighty places I would visit for business. I was on my way to Ann Arbor when he was relocated from the hospital to a rehabilitation clinic. Over the next week, he suffered a couple little strokes that went unnoticed. One impaired his peripheral vision, and the other his short-term memory. He had wanted to return home after leaving treatment, but by this point, he couldn't live alone.

I'm not sure where I was when my father went to an assisted living facility. The name is Springmoor. I finally saw it four months after his fall, when Hugh and I flew to North Carolina. It was early August, and we arrived to find him in an easy chair, blood pouring from his ear at an alarming rate. A nurse's assistant was dabbing at what appeared to be fake beet juice. "Oh, hello," my father said, his voice gentle and sleepy.

I assumed he didn't know who I was, but then he added my name and extended his hand. "David." He turned behind me. "Hugh." Someone had wrapped his head in gauze, and when he leaned back, he resembled the late English poet Edith Sitwell, who appeared distinguished and almost domineering. His brows were tiny and scarcely noticeable. It was the same for his lashes. I suppose, like the hairs on his arms and legs, they simply became tired of holding on.

"So, what happened?" " I inquired, even though I already knew. Lisa had informed me over the phone that morning that the grandfather clock he had bought to Springmoor had toppled on him. It was constructed of walnut and bronze and featured an abstract human face surrounded by numbers arranged at unusual angles. My mother always called it Mr. Creech, after the artist who created it, but my father calls it Father Time.

I told Hugh after hanging up with Lisa, "When you're ninety-five and Father Time practically knocks you to the ground, don't you think he's trying to teach you something? "

"He insisted on moving it himself," the woman trying to stop the blood explained, "and it cut his ear. We sent him to the hospital for sutures, but now it's started up again, maybe because he's on blood thinners, so we've phoned an ambulance." She turned to my father and raised her voice. "Haven't we, Lou? Haven't we phoned an ambulance? "

At that point, two EMTs rushed in, both young and bearded, like lumberjacks. Each took an elbow and helped my father stand.

"Are we going anywhere? He asked.

"Return to the hospital! " the woman exclaimed.

"All right," my father said. "OK."

They wheeled him out, and the woman said that the staff would remove bloodstains from the carpet, but it was the family's responsibility to remove them from any privately owned furniture. "I can bring you some towels," she volunteered.

A few moments later, another assistant entered the room. "Excuse me," she asked, "but are you the famous son? "

"I'm a pretty sorry excuse for being famous," I told her. "But yes, I'm his son."

"So you are Dave?" Dave Chappelle? Can I get your autograph? Actually, may I have two? "

"Um, sure," I replied.

I had just joined Hugh in cleaning the easy chair when the woman, who appeared little apprehensive around a world-famous comedian who is young, Black, and has his entire life ahead of him, returned for two more autographs.

"I'm the worst son in the world," I admitted, grasping for the shreds of paper mother was holding out. "My father fell on April seventh, and this is the first time I've visited, the first time I've talked to him, even."

"You put yourself down too much," the woman stated. "Just pick up the phone every now and then—that's what I do with my mother." She gave a forgiving grin. "You can make that second autograph for my supervisor." She then handed me a name.

The blood on our damp cloths looked even more artificial than the blood I'd seen fall from my father's ear. I took a few halfhearted swipes at the easy chair, but Hugh performed the majority of the work. I mostly glanced at the things my father had adorned his room with: Father Time, a number of streetscapes he and my mother had purchased in the 1970s, and rocks he'd brought back from fishing excursions, each with a date and the name of the river it had originated from written on it. I found it all quite gloomy. However, even a unicorn would have appeared dingy in this environment. I'm not sure whether it was the lighting or the height of the ceiling. Perhaps it was the hospital bed against the wall, or the floor-length curtains that appeared to have come from a funeral parlor. Down the corridor, a dozen or more residents, the majority in wheelchairs and some drooling over bibs, were watching M*A*S*H on television.

I couldn't help but think of Mayview, the nursing facility my father put his mother in in the mid-1970s. It felt like only yesterday that I went with him to see her. If I were to visit him in a comparable location, wouldn't I find myself in my own assisted care facility, the feeble widower reduced to a single room in the blink of an eye? Only I won't have children to care after me, the way my father had Lisa—who had been extraordinary—and my brother, Paul, and Amy and Gretchen. My sister-in-law, Kathy, had excelled everyone by visiting Dad twice a day, taking him to lunch, and putting lotion into his feet. I was the sole exception. Me. David Chappelle.

"Do you think we can take some photos together? "One of the nurses asked me on my way out.

"Oh, wait, I want one too," another woman added, followed by another.

"Look," I pictured them telling others later, "I got a photo of me with Dave Chappelle."

"No, you didn't," they would be informed.

Of course, I'd be gone by then. As always.

Hugh and I drove to our property on Emerald Isle—the Sea Section—after leaving Springmoor, and were joined a few days later by his older brother, John, who'd brought two boys: Harrison, his seven-year-old grandson, and Austin, Harrison's half brother, who was eleven years old. All three live in a little town on a strait some hours west of Seattle. The children had never seen water they could walk into without wailing from the cold. They had never seen fine sand or pelicans. I expected them to be overjoyed, but it was difficult to pry them away from the portable gaming device they had brought from Washington—a Nintendo Switch.

"What? Harrison cried, frustrated, after visiting the mansion. "You don't have a TV we can connect this to? "

He was one of those children who had bypassed cuteness and gone right to handsome. I suppose this could change over the following few decades: his nose could become out of proportion to the rest of his face. He could lose his chin or a cheek in an accident, but he'd still have cornflower blue eyes and a pouty, almost feminine mouth, with the bottom lip slightly larger than the top. He was the most attractive person in the room no matter where we went. Does he recognize this? I wondered. Kids his age are frequently unaware.

Looks aside, Harrison and his half-brother, who live with their mother, were far from spoilt. The Nintendo was something John had given them earlier in the year. They are not allowed to have one at home, and after a few hours, I understood why. The console was the first thing they reached for in the morning and the last thing they looked at before going to bed, which was usually after one a.m.

The guys did not seem to follow any rules as I did when I was their age. "You can't just leave the table," I told Harrison on the first night of his visit, as he finished his dinner and hurried off to play Minecraft. "You have to ask if you can be excused."

"No, I don't."

"No, I don't, Mr. Sedaris." I made the lads call me that and corrected them whenever they messed up. "I'm an adult and you're guests in my house."

"It's not your house, Hugh's," Harrison said.

Hugh glanced up from his plate. "He's correct. Look at the deed. "This place bears my name."

"Yes, well, I bought it," I replied.

Harrison rolled his eyes. "Yeah, right."

The next day, I came down from my desk to find him and his half brother playing video games on the sofa.

"Why don't you put down your Nintendo and write a letter to your mother? "I said.

Harrison nudged Austin in the ribs, saying, "Stranger danger." This was evidently something they'd learnt in school. "Don't talk to him."

"I'm not a stranger, I'm your host, and it wouldn't hurt you to be a little more like me for a change."

"What's so great about you? "Harris asked.

"Two things," I said, my thoughts racing as I tried to think of something. "I'm rich and I'm famous."

He shook his head and focused on his game. "I don't believe a word you say."

"Hugh! "I called. "Will you tell Harrison that I am rich and famous? "

"I think he's out on the beach," Austin remarked, his gaze fixed, like his half brother's, on the paperback-sized console they shared. "What did you do to become famous?" "

"Wrote books," I said.

"Well, I've never heard of any of them," Harrison explained.

"That's because you're seven," I explained, more hurt than I wanted to acknowledge. "Grown-ups recognize who I am. "Especially nurses."

Hugh noticed someone photographing our house later that afternoon, the fourth time in a week. "I think they read your last book," he joked.

"See! "I called to Harrison in the next room.

He was focused on his game and did not respond.

"They're most likely just taking pictures of the Sea Section sign," I told him. "It's a pretty good name for a beach house." I then told him about a place our neighbor Bermey had described further up the coast called YOU DIDN'T GET THIS, BITCH. "That probably gets photographed as well," I answered, "especially by divorced men."

The photography on the street side of our house paled in comparison to what was going on in the backyard. When I was younger, sea turtles would deposit their eggs on the beach, and no one bothered about it. Now, it's a big thing. Loggerheads appear on bumper stickers and signs. They are an attraction, similar to the wild horses at Ocracoke. The location where the eggs are laid is marked, and when the time comes for them to hatch, a team of Turtle Patrol volunteers is despatched.

A bright yellow stake had been driven into the sand near the foot of the wooden stairway that led from our house to the beach, and the morning after the boys arrived, volunteers dug a hole to help the hatchlings find the ocean. It was now lined on either side with folding chairs for Turtle Patrol nest-sitting. I told Hugh, "It's like the red carpet at the Academy Awards."

People going down the beach noticed the yellow caution tape and the trench, which was being patrolled by do-gooders dressed in bright Turtle Patrol T-shirts, and approached to ask questions, causing the gathering to grow. At night, they'd sit with infrared spotlights, peering down, waiting for the slightest movement, cameras ready.

"It's actually called a boil," Kathleen told me. "That's because when the eggs hatch and the babies claw their way to the surface, the sand churns."

"Isn't this exciting? " I explained to the boys.

"Uh-huh," they replied. "Sure."

"Really? "I said. "You aren't interested in nature?" "When I was that age, all I cared about was stealing and spying on others. I told them about the hideous-looking silver possum that had come up the front stairs of our house last Thanksgiving. "We fed her fruit and leftovers, and you should have seen how her hands grabbed the food, almost human-like. "Every night, she came."

Austin responded pleasantly but vacantly, "Wow."

The only way to grab the lads' attention was to throw one of the stink bombs I had purchased on Cape Cod a week before. I expected the scent to be minor—perhaps like an old sock—but it cleared not only the room where the boys were playing Mario Kart, but the entire side of the house. For the most part, it smelled like sulfur, similar to what I imagine Satan's bathroom might smell like after he'd spent some time on the toilet with the National Review.

"Goddammit," Hugh exclaimed, holding his nose and opening the front and rear doors, let hot, humid air in. "And we're expecting company! "

Harrison chastised the book writer. He was dressed in Minecraft pajamas and resembled a male model that had been reduced in size by a machine.

Austin was the more pleasant of the two brothers. He would ask inquiries and offer to help. His voice sounded old-fashioned, like a boy's in a radio serial. "Gee, willikers!" " You could imagine him saying that if it were the title of a video game in which objects exploded and women were shot in the back of the head.

Compared to other kids I'd known, the two were quite good. Both enjoyed fish and always finished everything on their plates. They rarely bickered, and when they did, it was over in a minute or two. There was no crying, and even better, no sulking. That's horrible for me. "Oh, move on, for God's sake," my mother used to say as we stared and stewed, promising never to forget the unfairness of egg salad or broken potato chips from the bottom of the bag.

The boys weren't really interested in the boil going on in the back of the house, but I figured they'd alter their views if they saw the newborn loggerheads. The eggs were the size of Ping-Pong balls and were expected to hatch on Monday. Then Tuesday. Then Wednesday. At night, we'd go to the top of our stairwell to observe if there was any activity. "Aren't we blessed to have front-row seats? "I would say.

"If you say so," Harrison would respond.

My fifteen-year-old niece, Maddy, has a similar attitude. She was at the beach as well, but you wouldn't know it. We saw her briefly at lunch and dinner, but she spent the rest of her time alone, her face six inches from her phone. Was there an analogous when I was younger? I wondered. I don't remember my parents weeping, "You and that goddamn transistor radio!" "

The boys slept in what we had come to refer to as my father's room. It was uncomfortable being at the beach without him, but we didn't have the necessary equipment: a walk-in shower, bars alongside the toilet, and so on. He didn't require those items a year ago, but that's the difference between 94 and 95. He drove to the gym the day before his fall, unaware that it would be his last time behind the wheel and his last night in his own bed. There would be a lot of stuff in his immediate future, including the last time he could dress himself and walk.

I was concerned that he was entering a period of death by a thousand cuts, with a fall, a stroke, and an accident with a grandfather clock. That's how it was with the other really elderly people I've met in my life: the woman across the street from us in Normandy, our next-door neighbor in London. Phyllis Diller. We met late in her life and became friends. She lived in a home in Brentwood, and every time I went there, she was a little less able—her eyes wouldn't stop watering, and she couldn't get up from a chair. Phyllis was fortunate to be able to stay at home and hire round-the-clock help, as well as to be famous—a legend by any definition. Throughout the day, disciples came to pay her homage, and she went out every night. Thus, she was spared the loneliness that so many elderly people experience.

When I last went to her house, I found her on the back patio. It was one in the afternoon, and she was sipping a martini. "Karla," she instructed her assistant, "get David something to drink." Would you like a vodka, sweetie? "

"Just some water," I replied, sliding in alongside her.

"Water with vodka?" "

"No, just the water."

"Bring him a vodka tonic," Phyllis said, apparently forgetting that I do not drink.

In Karla's absence, she pointed to two pigeons parading around her well groomed yard. "All those two do," she remarked, holding her glass with her blue-veined hand, the fingers as thin and brittle as twigs, "I mean all they do, is fuck."

We were off somewhere when most of the turtles hatched, some sixty-three of them. We also missed the six who managed to get away early the next morning. Hugh's brother left with the boys on Sunday, and a few hours later, the final one erupted. I was on a stroll at the time, and I returned minutes later, after it had stumbled down the trench and into the ocean. "It was heartbreaking," Hugh explained. He was standing in his swimming suit on the beach behind our house, one of perhaps fifty people.

"What was so sad? "I asked. "I mean, he made it, right? "

Hugh's voice cracked. "Yes but…he was just so…alone."

"I can't believe you missed it," he added before we went to bed that night. He had just taken off his shirt, and I took a moment to enjoy his tan. It wasn't something he worked for; it just happened, the result of all the hours he'd spent in the ocean, occasionally with the guys but mostly alone, swimming like some sort of beast, one moment on his back and the next on his stomach, spinning like a chicken on a spit. He's been doing this since he was a child, and as a result, his shoulders are so broad that my arms can barely fit over them. Still, I try. He slips under the blankets, and I cling to him like a barnacle, remembering all of the couples I know who no longer share a bed. "He snores. " the wife will tell me, or "I need my own space." I'd despise separate rooms, though a sleep apnea machine or incontinence may be a deal breaker. Definitely incontinence. I have no idea what awaits us on the other side of our late middle age, but I am certain it will not be good.

Before departing to England, we traveled back to Raleigh and ate lunch with my father, who was wearing a biscuit-sized bandage on his ear and using a walker with his name and room number inscribed in Magic Marker. I did not want to meet at Springmoor—"You said you were Dave Chappelle! "—so Lisa and Bob drove him to the café we had all decided on. As I watched him gently approach the table from a distance, I was struck by how fragile he appeared. Still, his spirits were high, and he was engaged, even humorous, especially when discussing Springmoor and how the staff may walk in whenever they want: "It's a problem because I don't always feel like wearing clothes, if you catch my drift."

"Sure," I replied, wondering what was wrong about underpants.

Kathy also met us at the restaurant, and around halfway through our meal, she informed my father about the newborn loggerhead turtles she had witnessed hatching on Emerald Isle a few days before.

"Oh, right," my father replied. "They've been laying eggs there for centuries. For even longer, I imagine. Eons."

"And the last one to spring up out of the sand," she recounted, "was the Turtle Patrol guys named Lou. That's quite amazing! "

A more sentimental audience could have placed their hands on their hearts and cooed. Eyes may have misted or filled with genuine tears. If someone had named a human kid after my father—say, Lou Sedaris Kwitchoff, or, better still, Louis Harry Sedaris Kwitchoff—my family could have shared a moment over our salads and sandwiches at the Belted Goat. But this was an endangered turtle with only a slim chance of survival till the end of the week, so it was more like to naming a bar of soap after someone, assuming soap could paddle around temporarily.

CHAPTER 3
ECCHYMOSE

When Hugh was in his late twenties, he purchased an old stone farmhouse in a small Norman village. It didn't cost much, but it also lacked amenities: no electricity or running water, and a roof that needed to be replaced. He took offense when I labeled it a dump, so I referred to it as a hovel, which I believe it technically was. The ground-level floor was made of hard-packed earth. The second floor had worm-eaten timber, as did the attic. The rafters, doors, and windows were all rotted. The previous owner had left an armoire, a table, and half a dozen barrels, some of which were large enough for me to stand inside. The apartment smelled like old rope, both upstairs and downstairs.

I first visited the hovel in 1992, a few years after Hugh and I met. I knew no French at the time, except for a few odd words like traffic congestion, raw, and the verb to shorten. And, of course, all the English terms that happen to be French: nocturnal. Surveillance. Cliché. I expected that the peasants would have learned something from watching American television, as Dallas was still rather large at the time. People were named their girls Pamela, but that was all they were willing to do at the time. So, throughout my first four visits, I spent the entire time smiling and seeming to understand what was going on.

Being stripped of my personality was quite humbling. I wasn't the sharpest guy in the room, but I could generally hold my own. In Normandy, however, I was seen as an imbecile. Worse, I couldn't laugh for the life of me. In America, that was my identity. I appeared on the radio and in periodicals. Now I was just a lump, and Hugh dominated all of the attention. He spoke and comprehended French fluently but couldn't be relied on to translate, especially when there were a lot of people around. When we received electricity and water, he began inviting pals around. Groups of ten would arrive for lunch, and I would feel so excluded. "What did she say?" " I once inquired after a guest had held the floor for a few minutes and then covered her face with her hands.

"She vomited on herself throughout her wedding. "I will tell you later."

I disliked being excluded, so between a little visit in May 1997 and a much longer one the following August, I enrolled in a ten-session private French class taught by a petite, sharp-nosed thumbtack of a woman. Elise was Canadian, and we met twice a week at the World Trade Center. Around the same time, I began opening my Larousse dictionary, writing random words on index cards, and memorizing them during my daily walks. "Why did you learn the word bruise?" She groused one afternoon. "When will that come in handy?" "

In retrospect, I believe I understand her argument. Why choose master bruise over, say, umbrella? But how many of us are aware of which words and phrases may be advantageous when learning a foreign language? It's like guessing the future.

If I had it to do over, I'd master the line "Let us go see what your grandmother is up to," but bruising was also useful that summer. Hugh and I had the main support beam in the living room replaced, which was a major task. While we were treating the new one for worms, I fell off my ladder and hit my thigh on a hefty chair. "Look," I said the next morning, pointing to the purple smudge on my skin. "A bruise!" "

I repeated it later that day to the woman across the street. Madame G was impressed, but she also corrected my pronunciation. "Ecchymose," she explained. "Pas ecchymuse." She and her husband were in their early 70s and raised horses and lambs. They also maintained bunnies and hens. They maintained Madame G's energetic, ninety-eight-year-old mother, Granny G, in the doll-sized house next to theirs, who had long white hair and went for walks through the forest every afternoon, collecting berries or mushrooms depending on the season. They also cared after Monsieur G's younger sister, Clotilde, who had Down syndrome and was extremely short. People with her disease usually die early, but she was in her mid-fifties. Clotilde wore heavy glasses, making her eyes appear smaller. She had gray hair and whiskers and spent her days standing up dominoes and knocking them down. When the weather was nice, she did it on a metal-topped table in her front yard, pausing only when Madame G barked, "Monte!" " This was her cue to climb the front stairs of the house, followed by another set to the second level, where the restroom located. Madame G stated to Hugh, with patience, that she would sit on the toilet till the end of time until someone told her to get off. She cared deeply for her sister-in-law.

Clotilde's only word I ever heard was huge, and it was in response to the same question: "Do you want a big slice of tart or a small one?" "

"Gros," Clotilde would moan, and everyone would cheer.

"Everyone" that summer frequently included Madame and Monsieur G's two adult children and six grandkids. Three belonged to their son, who worked for the electric business and had several badly drawn tattoos on his arms. Then their daughter gave birth to three boys. The middle child, Olivier, was twelve years old. I met him a year before, but he'd grown taller and now had two inches on me. Between one August and the next, he became secretive in the same way that I had when I was his age. I gathered he had discovered a secret—that he was gay. It's funny how that works. One moment you're a child, and all you know is that you're different from other boys. Then you become older and realize what that thing is.

If you go to a progressive private school and have supportive parents and a large circle of artistic friends, you might be able to go straight from realization to acceptance. Olivier's family appeared really cool. His grandparents had no problem with me and Hugh, or with the lesbian couple who eventually moved in down the road and were so butch that we all mistook them for men. But twelve is a tender age, especially in those pre-internet days, and even more so when you live, as Olivier did, in a town of only thirteen thousand.

Our tiny community had a population of about fifty people, with the most of them retired or well into maturity. There was no one for the kids to hang out with other than themselves and the inarticulate man-child—me—who lived just across the street. I spent a lot of time at the Gs that summer, aiming to enhance my French. At first, I didn't understand anything. Then one word, then two. "Viens…Intermarché?" one of the Gs would inquire. I'd get into their car and accompany them to the uninspiring Walmart-style hypermarket where they preferred to shop. It was the type of establishment that sold both scallions and riding lawn mowers, smelled like a brand-new beach ball, and was destroying small businesses across the country. "Why here?" I wanted to inquire, but the answer was obvious. Raising sheep was not a profitable endeavor. Hypermarkets sold products at lower prices and in larger quantities.

The grandchildren were present a lot that August, particularly Olivier and his cousin Claudette, who would go on to become nurses. We met in the Gs' tight dining room one night to celebrate her thirteenth birthday, and as the lights were turned off in preparation for the candlelight cake, I yelled out in a panicky, accusatory tone, "Mon portefeuille!" (My wallet!) I received my first chuckle in French.

"Do you want to take children to the river?" " Madame G proposed the next afternoon.

It wasn't far from her house, a ten-minute stroll across a paddock and into the woods. Claudette and Olivier talked to each other on the way.

I heard the words: beach, hot, Spain. Olivier and his family had just returned from there, all of them very browned. They were all quite attractive lads, with their mother's black hair and olive skin. At fifteen, the oldest was already attractive. His features were solidified while Olivier's were still in play, with the eyes a little too huge. They made his mouth look tiny and girlish. It was a doll's face flecked with moles, reminiscent of my own when I was his age.

Once we approached the woods, I spotted Olivier tripping and pulling onto me for support. I didn't think much of it the first two times. Then I realized it was just an act, an excuse to establish physical contact. He did the same as we crossed the river. The water was chilly and shallow, with enormous flat pebbles hardly a foot apart. A toddler half Olivier's age could have done it, but he kept pretending to lose his footing. Then he'd grab me in key places like my stomach, buttocks, and upper arms. His hands lingered, sensing me rather than simply providing support.

"Look! " he stated at one point. I turned to face him, and he pulled down his swimsuit, pointing to what appeared to be a mosquito bite on his bottom.

His cousin laughed, and I thought, "No! Put that away!"

A bit later, I noticed Granny G walking down the path with a basket of blackberries. "Bonjour! "I called in a way that said 'Help! —so loudly that birds took off.

When we returned to the Gs' house, Olivier's eyes sank and refused to see mine. There was no change in Claudette's behavior. She was her usual happy self, but when her cousin saw other grownups, I was dead to him.

That night, over dinner, I asked Hugh, "Can a twelve-year-old sexually harass someone? "

The next day, I was at home, writing in the milking parlor that I used as an office, when Olivier entered through the back door. "Hugh…here? "

I declined, and he hopped up the small staircase to our bedroom. "Are you two together?" He asked. That's what I assumed he was going at. To emphasize his point, he made fists and bumped them into each other. I was trying to figure out what to say when he wrapped his arms around me. If I hadn't moved my head so quickly, the kiss he planted would have landed just above my left ear instead of on my lips. It was totally unexpected—shocking. At the same time, I realized how this would appear to someone looking in through the window, and I wriggled away, saying, "Grandmother!" "When Olivier grabbed me again, I remembered those old New Yorker cartoons of the boss chasing his secretary around the desk. But in reverse. Additionally, the secretary is male. And a child.

When I told this incident to a friend back in New York, he wondered why I hadn't been more firm. "Why not just say, 'Look, this is inappropriate'? "

I stated that, properly speaking, the sentence—and the delicate ones that would follow—were beyond me. Then I remembered what it was like to be twelve and queer. You might grope a boy your age at a slumber party, pretending it was just for fun, but if he caught you, you'd deny everything and then set out to destroy him. "Me? You began it! "The shame and remorse are tremendous when you're a kid.

If I had embarrassed Olivier, he could have said anything. And who would the villagers believe? The cute twelve-year-old with the nice family, or the immigrant who speaks like a baby and is openly homosexual?

"Grandmother! " I repeated, sprinting out the front door, which we always left open. Everyone's was, regardless of how many flies they let in. A closed front door indicated that you were either sleepy or up to something.

For some reason, Olivier was only interested in me and not Hugh. Perhaps because I am smaller and closer to his size. In addition, I have never held any positions of power. Even first-graders do not always follow my instructions. I expected this to change as I got older, but it hasn't. No one is terrified of me.

I'm guessing Olivier watched the house until Hugh's car drove away and he realized I was alone, because he never came over else. I tried closing and locking the front door, but it didn't keep him from crawling through the window one afternoon. I was having a nap, and when I awoke to find him standing near the bed, I knew what was coming. "Grandmother!" I cried. But before I could stand, he was down on the mattress, almost in my lap, his pulse pounding so loudly that I could hear it and Clotilde's dominoes falling against the metal-topped table across the road.

I told Hugh that night, "What surprises me is his brazenness. I would never have been so daring when I was twelve, even if the other person was my age." I wondered if Olivier had had an encounter with a teacher, a coach, or simply a gay adult he'd met. I was forty-one that summer. That was ancient for a seventh student, but I could understand what he was going through. When I was his age, I would wait until everyone else in the house was asleep. Then I'd sneak into the family room, where my father would be asleep in front of the TV. He'd be in his undies, as usual, dozing in his chair, and I'd sit on the coffee table, examining him. Most of the time, I'd be wearing briefs with the back cut out with scissors. It's nothing I'm proud of; just the reverse. I feel ashamed just thinking about it. Even at the time, I wondered what on earth I was doing. I'm not sure what I expected to happen if my father woke up. It wasn't the sex I wanted. I'm not sure I grasped the mechanics back then, the what-went-where part. I guess I just wanted to cuddle. With my father. I was wearing underpants that I had cut the back of. And my brown-framed glasses.

Our family room was on the bottom floor and usually smelled like mildew. It was accessible from the outside via two sliding glass doors, and I always pondered what someone peering inside would think. This phase lasted only a few months, if that. And I did not do it every night. The next afternoon, I'd sit on the coffee table with my naked bottom, watching my sisters eat their cookies or potato chips, and I'd feel embarrassed of myself. I was utterly out of control that year. So, I knew, was Olivier.

I pondered visiting his grandparents with Hugh in tow to translate. But as a queer youngster, your biggest concern is that someone will expose you. That was not something I could do in good conscience. Again, if Olivier felt cornered, he might say anything. When I was eleven years old, a year younger than him, I developed feelings for Mrs. Haugh, a neighbor. I don't remember why I chose her above any of the other mothers on our block. She had a wonderful chuckle, I recall, and was always kind to me, asking questions and seemed to pay attention to my responses. Mrs. Haugh was chubby and had three, possibly four children. I began by leaving flowers outside her kitchen door, and then handcrafted cards. I'd sneak over early and wait until her husband—my rival—had left for work.

In early September, I flew back to New York, where I could speak and be acknowledged as a complete person. I didn't see Olivier again until the following August. By that time my French had improved, and he had outgrown me. "This kid's going to be a famous fashion designer," Madame G proclaimed, smiling in his direction as we sat around her living room one afternoon. "He is even taking sewing lessons, Olivier."

He grumbled yes and returned to the Game Boy he was playing with.

He never came to our house again, or even called me by name. I hadn't understood until then how terribly charmed I'd been by his attention the previous year, by the thought that no matter where I was or what I was doing, someone was thinking of me, possibly even missing me. Is this how a teacher feels when a student's crush fades?

The more French I studied, the more I understood how damaged the Gs' relationship was with their daughter, Olivier's mother, who eventually broke off contact with her parents and prohibited them from visiting their grandkids. Clotilde died, and Madame G's mother died not long after, at the age of 103. I saw Olivier a few years later, shortly before Hugh and I packed up and relocated to Sussex. He was working in his hometown, at the hypermarket that his grandparents used to drive me to. He was probably approximately twenty at the time, dressed in jeans and a polo shirt. Over this, he wore a synthetic red uniform jacket with short sleeves. I observed from a distance as he took the security tag off a pair of pants. Then he folded them, scanned a few groceries, and stared blankly into space as the client opened her purse and started looking for her credit card. His skin appeared sallow in the strong lighting that throws no shadows. He appeared empty.

Is that all? I pondered, almost irritated. No university, no relocation to a bustling city to become the next Mugler or Gaultier? Working as a cashier at Intermarché, of all places? Of course, I wasn't doing anything at his age. It was one of the worst years of my life. I dropped out of college, lived in my parents' basement, and spent my days getting high. Hopefully Olivier had simply paused, waiting at the gate for a moment before taking off. Still, as I walked out the door to where I had parked my bike, I realized how much more I wanted for this boy: not only Paris, but the entire globe.

I earned my bachelor of arts degree in 1987, when I was thirty.

Our commencement speaker was Vito Acconci, a conceptual artist. He'd accomplished a lot, but his most notable achievement was the construction of a wooden ramp at a New York gallery. Then he hid beneath it for several weeks, masturbating nonstop.

"You could do that! "My mother said when I told her who he was. "Isn't that the goal? Doing what you love while being compensated for it! "

I don't believe she understood a word of the man's commencement address. I'm not certain I did either. In preparation for today, I considered what he might have said that would have influenced my future.

I assumed my post-college life would be similar to the one I'd been living for the past decade: work some minor job that didn't require much thought, then return home and do my own thing. The majority of my friends and half of my family lived this way.

My sister Gretchen went to RISD to study art. Then there was Amy at Second City. And, boy, did our father give us hell about it. "Art or comedy is all well and good, but you need to find something to fall back on," he'd tell you.

I frequently hear this from parents when I meet them at book signings. "Our daughter is an aspiring writer, and we told her that's fine, but she needs to find something to fall back on."

"So she is a bad writer? " I ask.

"Well, no."

"Is she lazy? Has she exhibited no improvement since she began? "

"Of course not," the parents reply. "She is lovely. Writing is all she cares about.

"So why does she have to fall back? " I ask. "Are you saying you don't believe in her before she's had a chance to show herself? "

It's an unfair question on my part because it makes the parents appear unsupportive. They mean that they do not want their child to be broke or rejected. But there are many worse things. At twenty-two, you're predisposed to poverty and rejection. Do you know why? Because you look good. You may not realize it this morning, but thirty years from now, you will look back at images of yourself from this day and wonder, "Why didn't anyone tell me I was so fucking attractive?" You may be unable to see it right now because you are comparing yourself to the person next to you or two rows above. But you're stunning.

And let me tell you something else: when you're on your deathbed, or at least, say, sixty-one, the time you'll remember most lovingly will not be the day you bought your first Picasso artwork at Sotheby's, the small still life painted in 1921—am I alone in this? —but in the years following graduation, when you were initially living as an adult, everything seemed imaginable. Maybe nothing went as planned, but you were confident it would. You were most likely broke and living in a substandard apartment. But it was your apartment, and you looked good. I suppose I'm saying that the next few years could be the best of your life. Simply don't blow it.

But how? you're thinking. I was going to tell you not to hurry into anything. "Don't become an adult quite yet. Take a crazy gamble, and whatever you do, don't return to your hometown. Do not, especially, return to your parents' home.

But who am I to tell that to a twenty-two-year-old owing $120,000? I'm not sure your generation has the luxury of drifting across the globe, trying this for a time and then that. How can you discover yourself when, before you've even started, you find yourself in debt?

So there goes that advise.

Here, nevertheless, are a few things I can tell you:

One. You must use extreme caution when using scented candles. There are really only two brands worth having: Trudon and Diptyque. I cannot afford it! You are probably thinking. Not with my $120,000 debt for a degree in dance history. To this, I respond, "Fine. You'll just have to forego scented candles until you can buy Diptyque or Trudon, or until someone presents them to you."

Two. Choose one item to be deeply offended by—rather than the dozens, if not hundreds, that many of you are currently dealing with.

Three. Stand up for what you believe in, as long as I do too. I fully support those of you who want to ban assault rifles. Take to the front lines, give it your all, and do not give up until you win. However, you should not petition to have a Balthus painting removed from the Metropolitan Museum of Art because you can see the subject's underwear. The idea is to have less in common with the Taliban, rather than more.

Four. Be yourself. Unless you are an asshole. How can I tell if I'm an asshole? You are probably wondering. So, pay attention. Do others shun you? wash you get into a fight whenever you park your car or wash your laundry?

For example, I've been working with a group called Love Hope Strength over the last four years. What they do is persuade individuals to give bone marrow, and I enjoy that they let me tell ridiculous lies about them. "If you sign up," I assure my readers, "you will get to have sex with the most attractive member of the cancer patient's family—young or old, they cannot by law refuse you."

People do not donate bone marrow in theaters, of course. Rather, someone swabs the inside of their cheek and completes a brief form. Finding a match is rare, but it does happen. The cutoff age is fifty, so I inform the audience. Then I announce that anyone who registers with Love Hope Strength will be able to go right to the front of the book-signing line. This is how you attract donors. However, if I have two thousand individuals in the theater, fifty of them may grab the bait. That may not sound like much, but it is a good amount, and if you visit forty cities, it adds up.

So I'm in Napa, California, and this woman, maybe sixty-five, complains that I'm being ageist and that if I don't allow her cut to the head of the book-signing line, she'll sue the show's producer for discrimination. Now, this is a relatively tiny theater. I've had twenty folks sign up to donate bone marrow. I'd told the audience that it doesn't hurt and that they can have sex with the cancer patient's preferred family member while having the extraction. This is the worst deception of them, because the process is actually excruciatingly painful. Here are twenty people who are willing to put up with a lot of agony in order to maybe save the life of a complete stranger. That, to me, is true heroism. And this woman threatens to sue if I don't let her move to the front of the queue. She's turning her selfish desire to get home as soon as possible into a fight against injustice.

That's an asshole, and you never want to be one. I scribbled in her book, "You are a horrible human being." Of course, she laughed, believing I was kidding. That's the disadvantage of writing humor. People always assume you're kidding. "No, I really mean it," I informed her. "You're awful."

She laughed harder.

Five. Always be prepared with a few jokes. They're useful for casual gatherings and definitely don't hurt at job interviews, depending on the position you're applying for. Here's something my friend Ronnie told me that's current, short, and easy to remember:

It is nighttime, and a cop stops a car carrying two priests. "I'm looking for two child molesters," he informs them.

The priests reflect for a time. "We will do it! "They say.

Six. This final piece of advice is one that few of you will take, which is terrible because it is just as vital as what I taught you about scented candles. And it is this: send thank-you letters. On a practical level, it is simply common sense. People enjoy doing things for people who express gratitude. Say your grandmother sends you $100 as a graduation present. If she has eight grandchildren who are or will be in the same situation as you, I guarantee that yours will be the only thank-you card she receives—not an email, text, or Facebook post, but an actual letter with a stamp. And she'll treasure it. Then, a few months later, you can write again, informing her that you have spent the rest of the money she sent. "I was at Goodwill, buying a dress I can wear for my job interview tomorrow," you'd say. "The skid marks should come off after the first wash, and as for the underarm stains, I suppose we'll see. But while I paid for it, I thought of how nice you've always been to me, and how fortunate I am to have you in my life."

The chances of her sending you more money are roughly 80%. Not because you asked for it, but because you are thankful. I've spoken with employers that indicate that applicants who write a thank-you note following an interview rise to the top of the list. When I'm on a book tour, I write to everyone who interviews me, as well as the stores and media escort. You know who else does this? Nobody.

It's not because they aren't appreciative; they probably are. Rather, they assume that people will understand. They will, of course. Your grandmother is used to mailing you gifts and never hearing back. She believes he's busy while you lie around messaging someone in the next room about something you just saw on television.

But here's the thing: she's busy, too, but she takes the time to send you something. I am not trying to be a guilt-monger. I'm trying to help you. And who am I? A reasonably successful individual, with a Picasso artwork and a number of books under his belt, who will return home at the end of the day and write to Oberlin's president to thank her for this degree, which I did not earn but am extremely glad for.

CHAPTER 4
I'VE GOT YOU (TOO LATE)

*G*rowing up in North Carolina, it's difficult to become attached to a beach house when you know you're only there for a limited time. If the hurricane does not occur this autumn, it will most likely come the next. Florence was the one who took our position in September 2018. Hugh was distraught, and my only thought was, "What's with the old-fashioned names?" Irma, Agnes, Bertha, and Floyd sound like pinochle tournament finals. Isn't it time for Hurricanes Madison and Skylar? Where is Latrice, or Category 4 Fredonté?

Along the North Carolina coast, Florence was claimed to have given the word "namaste" a new meaning.

"Are you planning to evacuate? "

"Namaste."

Hugh and I were in London when the hurricane struck, followed almost immediately by a tornado. Our friend Bermey owns a house near us called the Dark Side of the Dune, and he went over to check on the Sea Section as soon as people were allowed back on the island. He found our doors wide open, blown open by the wind. A major portion of the roof had been pulled off, and the rain that had fallen in the days since had caused the ceilings on both stories to crumble in, the water trickling down into the carport as if the house were a sieve. Bermey shot photos that I was embarrassed to share. It appears that rats had been residing in the second-floor ceiling. So there were our mattresses, littered with currant-sized turds and tufts of bloated, discoloured insulation.

All inside drywall would need to be replaced, as would the roof, doors, and windows. We were left with a shell, essentially. If ours had been the only affected area, repairs would have been simple, but between the hurricane and the flooding, thousands of homes were destroyed or severely damaged—and that was only in North Carolina.

Fortunately, our other house was not severely damaged. It's next door to the Sea Section, and Hugh bought it in 2016 despite my protests. His reasoning was that if he didn't obtain it, someone would most likely demolish it and build the type of McMansion that has become the norm on Emerald Isle rather than the exception. The grandeur of these new houses was one thing—eight bedrooms were normal, spread across three or four stories—but what they came with, and what you really didn't want next door, was a swimming pool. "It happened to us ten years ago," lamented my friend Lynette, who owns an older, traditional-sized cottage up the street from us. "Now all we hear is, 'Marco! ' 'Polo! Over and over. "It's like torture."

Hugh purchased a property that is considered ancient by Emerald Isle standards, having been built in 1972. It's a four-bedroom single-story house on stilts that has been painted a carnal pink. It, like the Sea Section, is right on the beach, but unlike the Sea Section, it is rented out to tourists. Hugh initially used an agency, but he now handles it himself through a variety of websites. Our friend Lee across the street leases out his home, Almost Paradise, as do the majority of our Emerald Isle neighbors, and each has a story to tell: People leave with the cushions and coat hangers. People grill on the wooden decks. They bring dogs, regardless of whether you allow them, and little children, which means that all sorts of stuff get flushed down the toilets, including seashells, doll outfits, and dice. And, of course, they grumble about everything: the TV only has ninety stations! There's some paint missing from the picnic table!

Lee once received a comment from a renter stating, "I was shocked by your outdoor shower."

"I was thinking, How surprising can this be? "I mean, you're at the beach for God's sake," he told me. Then I went out to wash up, and when I touched the hot water handle, I was thrown across the room."

Hugh bought the second house with everything in it, and while the furniture is a little heavy on the white wicker, it's not bad. He drew the line at the artwork, however. It was typical of a beach house: garish photos of sailboats and sunsets, placards saying IF YOU'RE NOT BAREFOOT, YOU'RE OVERDRESSED, and OLD FISHERMEN NEVER DIE, THEY JUST SMELL THAT WAY.

Hugh could make a living as a professional forger because he is so good at copying paintings. So, for the rental house, he recreated a number of Picasso paintings, including La Baignade (1937), which depicts two naked women knee-deep in the water with a third person watching. The figures are abstracted, almost machinelike, and cement-colored, set against a sapphire sea and a similarly intense sky. Hugh did three others, all beach-related, and had a comment from a tenant who stated that while the house was pleasant enough, the "artwork" (she used quotes) was obviously not family-friendly. As a mother with young children, she had removed the paintings during her stay and stated that if the owner wanted her to return, he would have to reconsider his decor. As if those were Hustler centerfolds!

"Do you believe that woman? " Hugh stated, over a year after the hurricane, when we were on Emerald Isle for a week. It was August. The Sea Section was still under construction, so we stayed at the pink house, which he was calling the Pink House, for reasons I could not for the life of me understand. "It's just such a boring name," I said.

"It really is," my sister Gretchen confirmed. She arrived an hour before we did, dressed in a fudge-colored tankini. Her long hair is going silver, and was gathered in a burger-sized bun, not quite on the back of her head but not on top either. She had turned sixty earlier that week and appeared as if she were made of well-burnished leather—the consequence of age and vigorous, year-round tanning. The skin between her throat and chest had become crepey, and it bothered me to notice. I can't bear watching my sisters become older. It just seems cruel. They were all such gorgeous.

"Calling this the Pink House is just…nothing," she said.

Given that the property was near to the Sea Section, I believe the ideal names were Amniotic Shack or Canker Shores. Both were suggested by a third party and were significantly superior to what I had come up with.

"So what was that? Gretchen inquired, opening a cabinet in quest of a coffee cup.

"Country Pride, Strong Family Peppermill," I informed her.

"Not that again," Hugh remarked.

"It's not a pun, but I think it has a nice ring to it."

Hugh opened the refrigerator and grabbed for the garbage pail. Renters are not meant to leave things behind, but they do, and none of their condiments met his standards. "It sounds like you just went to the grocery store and wrote down words."

"That's exactly what I did," I explained.

"That's terribly bad. It's my house, and I'll call it whatever I choose.

"But—"

He flung a bottle of orange salad dressing in the trash. "But, nothing. "Butt out."

C-R-A-B, Gretchen said.

I nodded in agreement and made pinching movements with my hands.

Hugh's presence in my family might be challenging at times. "What's his problem?" " My siblings have all asked me at some point, generally when flopping down on my bed during a visit.

"Whose problem is this? "I always say, but it's only a formality. I know who they're talking about. I've heard Hugh rage at everyone, including my father. "Get out of my kitchen" is rather common, as are "Use a plate" and "Did I say you could start eating?" "

I'd like to remain loyal when they grumble about him. I'd like to say, "I'm sorry, but that's my lover of almost thirty years you're talking about." But I've always thought that my first duty is to my family, so I murmur, "Isn't it horrible? "

"How do you stand it? " they inquire.

"I do not know! " I say. Of course I do. I adore Hugh. Not the gloomy Hugh who smashes doors and yells at people—that one I tolerate—but he isn't always like that. He did just enough to build a reputation.

"Why were you yelling at Lisa? " I inquired the year three of my sisters visited us for Christmas at our home in West Sussex.

"Because she came to the dinner table with a coat on."

"So? "

"It made her look like she wasn't staying," he remarked. "Like she was going to leave as soon as her ride pulled up."

"And…? " I replied, even though I knew precisely what he was saying. It was Christmas dinner, and this is a slippery slope. One year you sit at the table in a down coat, the next you're in a sweat suit, eating cold spaghetti out of a pan in front of the TV. My sisters might say whatever they want about Hugh's moodiness, but no one can accuse him of letting himself go or even of cutting corners, especially at the holidays, when everything is homemade, from the eggnog to the piglet with an apple in its mouth. There's a tree, there's his German great-grandmother's cookies, and he'll spend four days in an apron listening to "Messiah," and that's the way it is, goddammit.

Similarly, he creates the desired atmosphere at the beach. A few years ago, he created a spiral-shaped outdoor shower at the Sea Section, which we used even in the winter. He barbecues seafood every night and serves lunch on the balcony, which overlooks the ocean. He makes us ice cream from fruit sold by the growers at an outside stand and mixes beverages for cocktail hour. It's just that he is Hugh.

When I feel furious at someone, it is usually because of anything he or she said or did. Hugh's rage is more like the weather: something you open your door and walk out into. There is no dressing for it, and there is no way to predict it. A few months after we met, for example, he and I ran into an old friend at a play. This occurred in New York in 1991. We planned to go out to eat, but Hugh offered to cook at his apartment. Between the theater and Canal Street, his mood deteriorated. There was no cause. It was like the wind was changing direction. Dinner preparation involved a lot of muttering, and when my friend sat down to eat, his chair gave way, causing him to fall to the floor.

I apologized, saying the chair was already broken, but Hugh disagreed: "No, it wasn't."

"Why are you saying that? " I inquired after my friend had hobbled home.

"Because it wasn't broken," he replied.

"It doesn't matter," I clarified. "The point was to make him feel less embarrassed."

"Too bad," Hugh remarked. "I can't hide who I am."

"Well, it's really important to try," I informed him. "I mean, like, really, really important."

"Let me ask you two a question," Hugh remarked to Gretchen and me on our first afternoon at the Pink House that August. He opened the sliding glass door to the terrace and encouraged us to relax on the rocking chairs out there. The nails that held them together had been oozing rust onto the unpainted wood for so long that I put a towel down so as not to stain my white shorts, and got shouted at for it.

"Now, please."

I took a seat. "Ready."

"OK, do you think those are rickety? "That's what the renter who despised the paintings called them."

I settled in and swayed both side to side and back and forth. "Yes," I answered. "Rickety is probably the best word for this, possibly followed by kindling."

"This one, too," Gretchen replied.

"Well, you're just spoiled," Hugh said. "There's nothing wrong with those rocking chairs." He went back inside, and I heard the click that indicated he had locked us out.

"Goddammit," Gretchen exclaimed. "My cigarettes are in there."

Lisa, Paul, and Amy were unable to make it to the beach this time. It was awful to be on the island without them, but at least Hugh had less people to crab at. "If you want to raise your voice to someone, you might consider the contractors," I murmured in the living room the next morning, glancing next door at our vacant driveway and not hearing what I heard from other houses: the racket of hammers and saws.

Why don't you phone them? Hugh inquired. "I completed all the insurance forms. I handle all the bills and taxes, so how about you take care of something for a change? "

I did not answer, instead sighed, knowing he was not serious. Hugh doesn't want me to take care of anything. I would not have noticed him if Gretchen hadn't been present. I don't enjoy seeing my relationship through her eyes. That being said, I enjoy viewing my family from Hugh's perspective. To him, we're like flypaper dolls, all connected and speckled with filthy little corpses.

"What's with men constantly tweaking their balls? " Gretchen inquired, looking down at her phone.

"Are you referring to someone specifically? Hugh inquired.

"The guys I work with," she explained. "The landscape teams. "They can't keep their hands off their crotches."

"It could be due to heat rash," I said, noting that touching your balls in public is now forbidden in Italy. "Men did it to ward off bad luck, apparently."

"Hmmm," Gretchen remarked, returning her attention to her phone. "I was in a meeting a few weeks ago, and when I took off one of my shoes, a roach came out. It must have been hidden within when I got ready that morning."

What does that have to do with anything? Hugh inquired.

I rolled my eyes. "Does it matter?" "There's always time for a good story."

"Your family," he said, as if we were awful news.

That afternoon, I watched him swim into the ocean. Gretchen and I were on the beach together, and I remembered a young woman who'd had a leg and a few fingers amputated earlier that summer. Squinting toward the horizon as Hugh shrank, I stated that if the sharks caught him, I prayed they spared his right arm. "That way he can still kind of cook and access our accounts online."

It's difficult to see Gretchen's boyfriend crabbing at anyone. She and Marshall have been together almost as long as Hugh and I have, and I can't imagine a nicer guy. The same may be said for Paul's wife, Kathy. My brother-in-law, Bob, can be irritable from time to time, but when he screams at Lisa for, say, balancing a glass of grape juice on the arm of a white sofa, we normally think, Well, she deserves it. Amy has been alone since the mid-1990s, but I never heard her previous lover, a humorous and gorgeous asthmatic, rage at anyone, even when he had a good reason to.

Gretchen and I had hardly been on the beach for twenty minutes when she finally did what she always does. "I went online recently and read all sorts of horrible comments about you," she added lazily, as if the shape of a passing cloud reminded her of something.

I'm not sure where she got the idea that I—or anyone—would want to hear comments like these. "Gretchen, there is a reason I don't Google myself. I honestly don't—"

"A lot of people just can't stand you."

"I know," I replied. "It's the result of putting something out there—you're going to receive reactions. That doesn't mean I have to respect them all.

Jeez, I thought, rushing back to the house over the burning sand and wondering which was worse: being shouted at by Hugh or having to endure what Gretchen was dishing out. While I do not read reviews or look up myself, I do respond to emails. A few months ago, I received 230 letters addressed to my publishing business. I had previously responded to 180 and brought the remaining 50 to the beach, where I expected to see 10 per day. Most were just what I'd hoped for: pleasant messages from strangers. However, a complaint would occasionally arise. I'd want to say that I brush them off, and I suppose I will, in time. However, I will be plagued for days, if not months. For example, a woman sent me her ticket stubs and parking receipts, requesting that I reimburse her. She and her husband had gone to a reading and allegedly objected to my stuff. "I thought you were better than that," she chided, which always perplexed me. First and foremost, better than what? A clean show is acceptable, but it is not superior than a filthy one. Personally, I prefer a nice balance.

Putting that aside, who doesn't like to hear about a man who jammed a coat hanger up his ass? How could you not find that fascinating? "What kind of person are you?" "I wanted to write back.

After a long day of responding angry letters or emails, having an essay rejected, or hearing Gretchen tell me how much a woman she works with thinks I'm terrible, I'll go to Hugh and urge him to say something positive about me.

"Like, what?" " He'll ask.

"I shouldn't need to inform you. "Think about something."

"I can't right now," he will reply. "I'm in the middle of making dinner"—as if I had asked him to list all of the world's capitals alphabetically. I feel like I'm constantly complementing him. "You look so handsome tonight." "What a great meal you made." "You're so smart, so well-read," and so on. It's truly effortless.

"I don't want to give you a fat head," he'll say when I ask for something in exchange.

"My head is about the size of an onion. I urge you, please increase it."

He claims I've already received enough accolades. But it is not the same thing.

"OK," he'll say eventually. "You are persistent. How is that? "

I enjoy coming to Emerald Isle in May. It's not too hot, and most of my family can take a week off. The same holds true for Thanksgiving. However, August is something I do as a sacrifice for Hugh. The heat that month is unbearable, and the humidity is so intense that my glasses fog up. At home in Sussex, I'd cheerfully walk twenty-two miles each day, but on Emerald Isle at the height of summer, I'm lucky to get in fifteen, and even then I have to force myself.

I don't like to travel aimlessly, especially in an area where thunderstorms can strike without notice. I need a destination, so I usually head to a coffee shop near the grocery store, armed with a few letters to answer. I'll walk back and forth several times a day. Hugh and I lived in Normandy, and he overheard a local woman telling a friend about a mentally handicapped man she frequently saw marching past her home. She mentioned that he used headphones and looked at photographs while talking to himself.

Of course, that was me, but I wasn't holding any pictures. They were index cards with the day's 10 new French vocabulary terms on them.

Not long ago, in Sussex, an acquaintance approached me and told me a similar story. Again, I was labeled as mentally handicapped, this time because I was picking up trash and muttering to myself. I wasn't muttering, though; I was repeating sentences from my Learn to Speak Japanese, Swedish, or Polish audio program. "The woman who saw you said, 'I just hope no one tries to take advantage of him,'" my acquaintance explained.

On Emerald Isle in August, I was murmuring German. I might have picked up a few pieces of trash, but I wasn't carrying any equipment, just ziplock bags of hot dogs or thick-cut bologna to feed the snapping turtles in the canal.

We had been at the beach for four days when I spotted a large number of ant colonies in the dirt bordering the sidewalk between the strip malls housing CVS and the grocery store. The ants were cinnamon-colored, and hundreds of thousands of them raced around looking for anything to eat.

That afternoon, I said, "Excuse me," to the guy behind the hardware store counter. "I'd want to feed some ants and was wondering what you think they'd appreciate? How do they feel about bananas? "

The man's cheeks and neck had deep creases from age and exposure to the sun. "Bananas? " He removed his glasses and then put them back on. "No, I'd go with candy." Ants enjoy it very well."

I bought a bag of gummy worms next to the register, bit them in thirds, and, on my way back home, distributed them as evenly as I could among the various colonies. It made me pleased to think about the workers presenting sugar to their hungry queens and possibly being paid for it.

"Are you out there feeding ants candy? " Hugh commented that night at the table, while we were all reviewing our days. "They don't need your help, nor do the stupid turtles." You mess these things up by feeding them—you injure them." It wasn't what he said that bothered me, but his tone, which I would have missed if my sister hadn't been around.

"Well, they seemed pretty happy to me," I explained.

Gretchen patted my hand. "Do not listen to Hugh." "He knows nothing about being an ant."

This was a quick beach vacation. Renters were arriving on Saturday, so the three of us needed to tidy the house and leave by 10 a.m. Gretchen went a little earlier than we did, and while I was sad to see her go, it was a relief to be free of her judgment about the life I'd established with Hugh. As it was, whenever something positive happened that week, whenever he was cheery or thoughtlessly kind, I wanted to say, "See, this is what my relationship is like—this! "

It took three hours to go to Raleigh. I needed to get some work done, so I sat in the back seat while Hugh drove. "Just for a little while," I said. I must have fallen asleep, however. After waking up, I read for a few minutes before realizing the car wasn't moving. "What is going on?" I inquired, too lazy to sit up and look out the window.

"I don't know," Hugh replied. "An accident, maybe."

I regained my balance and was about to climb into the front seat when Hugh approached and tapped the car ahead of us. "Now look what you made me do! "

"Me? "

I know little about vehicles, but the one he hit was larger than ours and white. The driver appeared heavy and angry off, with huge, watery eyes that I would expect to see behind glasses. "Have you just hit me? " He asked, stepping towards us. He bent to examine his bumper, which appeared to be made of plastic and had a pale stain on it, presumably left by us.

Hugh rolled down his windows. "I maybe did, but just a little."

The man glared at what he undoubtedly imagined was an Uber driver earning extra money by driving people to the airport or wherever the gap-toothed junkie in the back seat was going. He checked his bumper again, and then the traffic began to move. Someone honked, and the man got back in his car. "Hit him again," I told Hugh. "This time, however, it will be more difficult. We need to show him who the boss is."

"Could you please shut up? " he stated. "As a favor for me. Please."

When we initially learned that Hurricane Florence had nearly devastated the Sea Section, I felt nothing. I expected this to happen, which contributed to my indifference. It was inevitable. Also, I wasn't as attached to the place as Hugh was. I was not the one who would be calling the insurance company. I would not drop everything to fly to North Carolina. I wouldn't be collecting turds from our mattresses or looking for a contractor. In that way, I could afford not to feel anything. After seeing the photos Bermey had given, I shrugged and went for a walk. I returned at dusk to find Hugh curled up in our bedroom, face in his hands. "My house," he wailed, his shoulders trembling.

"Well, one of your houses," I replied, remembering Florence's past victims. Some, like Hugh, were crying on their beds, distant from the devastated region, while others were on foldout sofas, sleeping bags, in the back seats of automobiles, or on cots arranged like circuits in public-school gymnasiums. People who felt they were far enough inland to be safe, with actual stuff in their now-demolished homes: items they treasured and couldn't replace. The most severely affected victims lost actual people—mates, friends, or family members carried away and swallowed by floodwaters.

However, this was a recurring theme for Hugh. Many of the houses he had grown up in had been destroyed, including those in Beirut, Mogadishu, and Kinshasa. He's actually quite unlucky in that regard.

I wrapped my arms around him and murmured what was expected of me: "We'll rebuild, and everything will be fine." Better, in fact. You'll see." This was how I pictured myself in a relationship: as the provider, the rock, the reassuring voice of wisdom. I had to stop myself from saying, "I've got you," as people do on TV when they're holding a distressed individual. It's a good sentiment, but culturally speaking, there was only a five-minute window when you could say it without looking lame, and that has already past.

I still have him, though. The two of us may appear incomprehensible to others, but the opposite is also true. I don't understand why a many of my friends are in long-term partnerships. But, what do I know? What about Gretchen, Lisa, or Amy? They watch me being punished and shut out of my own home on occasion, but where are they in the darkened rooms when a close friend dies or rebel forces raid the embassy? What happens when the wind picks up and floodwaters rise? When you realize you'd give anything to stop the other person from harming you, even if it meant tearing your head off again? You may forgive and forget again. Onward and upward, hopefully. Then it goes on and on.

CHAPTER 5
GOD AND THE NAIL AD

When I went to Chicago in 1984, one of the things that most excited me was the main branch of the public library, which looked like a palace and was loaded with tale collections that I would never have found back in Raleigh. Another pleasant surprise was my local bookstore, which was conveniently located near my apartment and regularly sponsored author events. It was exciting to literally sit at the feet of writers that I adored. I couldn't afford hardcovers, so I'd usually wait in line with a paperback, wondering, "What will I say?" Everything I thought of sounded ridiculous, and by the time I got to the signing table, I was always stuttering.

The friendliest of these authors would notice my shaky hands and go out of their way to make me feel better. It wasn't that difficult on their part—a simple query and a comment. "Do you live around here?" " "Those shoes appear to be handcrafted. Are you a cobbler? " Others would merely look up and nod as I rambled on. Then I would thank them before fleeing, my cheeks blazing.

My worst encounter still enrages me after all these years. I waited in line, nervous, and when I got up there, the author was talking to someone, possibly her publicist. "I don't know," she replied, sounding bored. "There isn't much to do in this town." Why don't you call Jerry and ask what he thinks? "My copy of her memoir was grabbed for, signed with only her name, and then pushed back. She did not even look up.

In that situation, I did not depart feeling ashamed. I left feeling betrayed. What I desired more than the book—which I would now rather die than read—was to be seen by this individual. If only for a few seconds. I left the store determined that if it was ever my turn to sit at that table as the author, I would engage them until they were old, or at least thirsty. "Okay, then," they'd say, glancing beyond me for the nearest exit, "let me let you go."

I would observe them till they withered.

And that is pretty much how things go. I usually start the discussion right away—that way the person requesting a book signed never has to say the things they agonized over while standing in line and will most likely regret later. There are exceptions, however. I was in Baton Rouge in late May 2013 when a woman approached and said, before I could catch her off guard, "You got me to put my bra back on."

I set down my pen. "I beg your pardon?" "

"I take it off the second I get home from work, and that usually means it's off for the night," she explained. "It means I'm not going anywhere for any reason. Then a buddy called to say you were coming, so I put it back on and hurried over to meet you! "

"Thank you," I said.

The following evening in Atlanta, I retold the woman's story in the hopes of receiving a positive response. It did, but the laughter were more of recognition than astonishment. "Do you remove your bra the instant you return from work? I asked the first person in line. She was large-breasted, with short, pewter-colored hair, and she placed her book on the table, saying, "Baby, I'll take it off before I get home."

"At the office?" "I asked.

"No," she replied. "In the car."

"Do you take off your blouse?" "

"Ain't no need to do that," she said. "What you do is unhook it in the back and then pull it out your sleeve."

"Is it off for the night once it's turned off?" "

"You know it is," she admitted. "A friend will phone inebriated, asking for a ride, and I'll answer, 'Honey, I took my bra off. "Get yourself a taxi."

The next in line was a guy college student. "I can always tell when my mom borrows my car because she leaves her bra in the glove compartment."

I believed this was simply an American phenomena, but when I started my UK tour, I realized I was mistaken. "Once this comes off, I'm in for the rest of the evening," women told me in London, Manchester, and Liverpool. I completed sixteen events. The last one was in Edinburgh. "Do you take off your bra on your way home from work?" "I questioned a young woman with orange hair.

She nodded.

"In your car?" "

"Oh no," she explained. "I do it on the bus."

This has been going on all around me for generations, and I was completely unaware. I grew up with my mother and four sisters!

It's not as if the clues weren't there. How many times have I knocked on a woman's door after dark and had her answer in a sweater that didn't match the rest of her attire, or with her arms crossed over her chest? I assumed that was sign language meaning "Couldn't you have told me you were coming?" " Now I see that it actually meant "If you think I'm putting my bra back on for this garbage, you are severely mistaken."

When I'm lucky, while on tour, a theme will emerge. It cannot be something I force. Rather, it should be organic. Bras were featured in one book, while jokes appeared in the next. It began with one, as a trucker called Bill Mooney informed me:

A Jewish man named Saul Epstein has a highly successful nail company, and when he retires, he gives it over to his son-in-law. Then he moves to Florida, and one day, while reading the New York Times, he stumbles across a full-page advertisement. It depicts Jesus hanging on the cross, with the words THEY USED EPSTEIN NAILS beneath him.

The old man is furious and reaches for his phone. "Are you out of your mind?" That is no way to offer our product! "

The son-in-law promises to solve things, and a week later, Epstein opens his Times to see another full-page advertisement. This one depicts a cross standing empty on a mountaintop. Jesus Christ is in front of it, lying face down in the dust, and two Roman soldiers on either side, looking down at him, with the words THEY DIDN'T USE EPSTEIN NAILS.

I repeated the joke in a bookstore that night and received the following:

What's the worst thing you can hear when playing Willie Nelson?

"I'm not really Willie Nelson."

And: It's late at night, and a man is about to go to bed when he hears a knock on the door. He opens it and finds a snail. "Yes," it responds; "I'd like to talk to you about buying some magazine subscriptions."

The man, overcome with wrath, rears back, kicks the snail as hard as he can, and goes off to bed.

Two years later, there's another knock. The man responds, and he finds the snail, who looks up at him and asks, "What the fuck was that all about? "

The next evening, in another bookstore, a man approached and said, "So God tells Adam, 'I'm going to make you a wife, a helpmate, and the most beautiful lady who has ever lived. She'll be great in bed, uncomplaining and adventurous. The trouble is, it will cost you.

"How much?" Adam asks.

"'An eye, elbow, collarbone, and your left ball.'

"Adam pauses for a moment before asking, 'What can I get for a rib?"'"

This was countered an hour later with: Three pals married three women from all across the world. The first chooses a Spanish girl and informs her on their wedding night that she is responsible for doing the dishes and laundry, as well as keeping the house in order. It takes some time to break her in, but on the third day, he returns home to find everything as he expected.

The second man marries a Thai girl. He instructs his wife to do all the cleaning, cooking, and ironing. He sees no results on the first day, but the next one is better. On the third day, he discovers that his house is clean, the dishes are done, and supper is on the table.

The third man marries an American girl. He instructs her to keep the house clean, the dishes washed, the yard mowed, and hot meals on the table every evening. The first day, he sees nothing. On the second day, he sees nothing. But by the third day, part of the swelling had subsided. He can see basic forms with his left eye, and his arm has healed enough to prepare a sandwich and load the dishwasher. He still has problems urinating.

Not everyone was skilled in their delivery. "OK," a person may reply, "a priest and a rabbi, or no…wait, a witch doctor and a priest and a rabbi go to a…oh gosh, just give me a second…"

By the end of the month, I had about 200 jokes, some of which were unworthy of repetition and others of great value. I saved them to a file on my computer and subsequently classified them, later noting a substantial overlap between sex and misogyny. Also, who knew there were so many pedophilia jokes? Everyone seemed to have a secret.

My next book tour was about monkeys, and the most recent one was about stuff that guys insert within themselves and then have to be extracted at the emergency room. This began when an ER nurse told me about a guy she'd seen earlier that week who had inserted a dildo too far up his ass. The door had closed behind it, so he attempted fishing it out with a coat hanger. When it proved to be the incorrect tool for the job, he severed it with wire cutters before tackling both the dildo and the cut-off hanger with a stronger, new hanger. Doctors and nurses frequently witness patients shoving light bulbs, shampoo bottles, or pool balls inside themselves and inventing elaborate stories to explain their situation. "I tripped" is a big deal.

And, yes, I'm somewhat clumsy. I trip all the time, but I've never gotten back on my feet with a pepper grinder up my ass, not even close. I'm very confident I could fall down all the steps in the Empire State Building, naked, with a greased-up rolling pin in each hand and a box of candles around my neck, and still wind up in the lobby with an empty rectum.

Another typical excuse is, "I accidentally sat on it." This implies that you were naked at the time and the can of air freshener, which happened to be coated in Vaseline, traveled all the way up inside you. "I must have left it on the sofa when I returned home from work and took a shower. Then I sat down to watch the news like I always do, and you know the rest."

A week into my tour, after I related the story onstage, a nurse handed me an X-ray of a man's pelvis with hand weights in it. How on Earth? I reflected, considering how much work it must have taken. And to follow up with a second? Who does this? Days later, I discovered an X-ray of a Bose speaker inside someone. "And it was still connected to Bluetooth," the woman who presented it to me said quietly.

June's parallel theme was money. On a book tour, you are usually accompanied by a media representative. This is the person who picks you up from the airport and drives you to all of your interviews and appointments. In Milwaukee, it was Mary. She's a handsome woman, perhaps a few years older than me, and we were on our way to my hotel when she mentioned a church-sponsored event she had attended earlier that day. "There was a speaker, and at the end of his talk, he gave everyone in the room a crisp new fifty-dollar bill and told us to go out into the world and pass it on to someone who needed it." She pulled her blond hair off her shoulder and checked her rearview mirror. "Oh, and it needs to be completed by 3:16. That corresponds to a Bible verse, but I can't recall which one.

Mary had a few hours between dropping me off at my hotel and returning at 5:00 to drive me to the bookshop, but she assured me that she would not be around any impoverished people between now and then. "So, if it's not too much effort, could you just pass the fifty on for me? "

I couldn't imagine a nicer way to spend the afternoon. Starting out, all I knew was that I did not want to give the money to a beggar. Better, I reasoned, to give it to someone who was doing a bad job. So I went in search of a McDonald's, planning to present the bill to the roughest-looking employee I could locate. "Excuse me," I would say. "Are you poor? Are you in debt? "

I hadn't brought my phone and had no idea where to find a McDonald's, so I just wandered. A half-dozen blocks from the hotel, I discovered a Subway, but I can't stand the scent of those places. I still had an hour till 3:16, but I wanted to spend as much time as possible in my luxurious hotel room before heading to the bookstore. OK, I thought, looking at my watch, a beggar will enough.

But then I didn't notice any; isn't that generally the case? When you just want to be left alone, they are everywhere and quite aggressive. Portland, Oregon's are the worst. They're all tattooed and laid out on the sidewalk. They were eighteen or twenty years old, with pierced noses and ears so full with holes that you could probably pull off the outer rims like a stamp off a sheet. "Asshole," they spit as you walk past, your gaze averted. "Go fuck yourself."

I'd have welcomed a tough young Portland beggar in Milwaukee, but everyone I saw appeared to be middle-class, if not wealthy—all on cell phones and carrying shopping bags. I noticed an exhausted-looking man with a pillowcase standing on a corner but backed away when he brought a can of beer to his lips.

No drinking, I reasoned, sounding like a holy lady.

By this point, it was 2:58, and I was beginning to panic, believing that if I didn't give the money away by 3:16, the God I profess not to believe in, the one whose only son was used to sell nails in one of my favorite jokes, would strike me.

When I saw the library, I thought, Bingo. That's poor-person central, at least in the United States, where similar places also serve as homeless shelters. This was a historic branch, and the building was impressive. Inside, it was cool and tomb-like. I observed two young ladies in their early twenties standing at the information desk, but everyone else was sitting—mostly slumped—with knapsacks and duffel bags on the floor beside them. No one was reading persuasively. The books appeared to be more of a prop, something to stare into, in the same way that my father would stare at magazines, turning to the same page for hours on end.

I walked up to the counter. "How can I help you?" a librarian inquired. She had a slightly severe expression and a longer-than-average neck, just like a librarian.

"This might sound unusual," I told her, "but I have fifty dollars to give to a poor person by 3:16. I notice some promising people here and was hoping you could guide me to the most in need."

The two young women standing nearby appear to have listened in.

"Give it to me," one of them requested. She wore a lot of foundation, and her brows resembled sketches. "I want fifty dollars." She was wearing a white T-shirt embellished with plastic diamonds. Because of the notebooks she and her friend were carrying, I assumed they were community college students, perhaps specializing in not giving a fuck.

If a stranger had approached me with a fifty-dollar bill when I was in college, I would never forget it. In the mid-to-late 1980s, that was a lot of money, one-quarter of my rent, but I would have probably spent it on luxury items—pot, most certainly, and some decent groceries, which at the time meant Marie's salad dressing. It arrived refrigerated in a jar and was sold with the lettuce at a store named Treasure Island. I would have purchased Green Goddess or Creamy Ranch. Then I'd gone high and dipped objects in my treasured dressings.

More than the pot and supplies, I would have loved a brief respite from the incessant worry I felt. Was there a single moment when I wasn't concerned about money? When wasn't I worried that a check might bounce or that a higher-than-average phone bill would force me to eat pancakes for a week? I don't recall buying anything impulsively. If chicken backs or cartons of spaghetti were ten cents cheaper five miles away, I'd ride my bike there in subzero temperatures. Meanwhile, I'd see individuals as poor as, or poorer than, me at the costly corner stores, purchasing milk and bread with food stamps. They didn't know how to shop since they hadn't been trained the same way my sisters and I were by a father who clipped coupons and bought all of our vegetables from what amounted to a purgatory bin, the one where things were dumped just before they went to the dumpster. All of our canned foods were dented and off-brand. Some labels contained only one word, such as BEANS or CORN.

I could understand how the girl behind the counter might have needed the money. The difficulty was that she had asked for it. People like to claim, "Asking doesn't cost a thing," or, "If you don't ask, you don't get." But I believe it's overrated—your reward for being pushy, rather than being fascinating or deserving. Do I think this way because I can't ask for things? I wondered. Have I spent the afternoon hunting for the youthful, hapless version of myself, the one I was before my luck changed?

"Give it to me," the young woman said, her tone becoming more aggressive.

"Let me put you in touch with our security guard," the librarian said. "She'll be able to help you much better than I can."

It was eight minutes past 3:00.

"I need fifty dollars," the college student reiterated. "I want it."

Her friend then chimed in. "Me, too. "Give it to me."

What point does this constitute robbery? I wondered.

The security guard was in her seventies and fragile. Her uniform featured short sleeves and showed her twig-thin arms, which resembled a snowman's. Who do you call if you're in trouble? I thought. The woman has all the authority of a crumpled leaf.

"Are you seeking for someone poor? " She looked through her large glasses on the far side of the room. "We received a lot of them today. But, what about him? "

She raised her chin to a sorrowful-looking man in his sixties whom I had previously seen. Aside from his duffel bag and his unconvincing reading style, I'd noticed how bad his hairdo was. It seems he had done it himself with a campfire.

I stepped up to him. "Excuse me."

He either couldn't hear or ignored me.

"I apologize for bothering you," I shouted slightly louder. "Could you just take this for me? "

I placed fifty dollars on the table beside him.

"Sure," he replied, as if he was doing me a favor.

The young woman at the counter narrowed her gaze. "Shit."

Her friend suggested a slight variation. "Shithead."

I thought I was done. And with six minutes to spare. Take it, God.

"It was actually really smart of that speaker to hand out fifty-dollar bills," I said Mary when she arrived to take me to the bookstore. The afternoon had almost made me high, and words flowed out of my mouth like water from a fire hose. "It made me reflect on a variety of topics, including how fortunate I am, how I judge others, and the arbitrary rules we set. Additionally, it makes for an intriguing story. You're an asshole if you give away $50 of your own money and tell anyone about it. I mean, the one thing you can't talk about in this world is your generosity. Because the moment you do, generosity ceases to exist; by exposing it, you have destroyed it. Plus, it makes the individuals you tell feel ungrateful, and they end up disliking you."

Mary nodded.

"And there's no point in me doing anything if I can't write about it," I said. "It would be like…walking ten miles without my Fitbit on—a complete waste. I mean, I do do things I don't put to paper: I use the restroom, I have sex. But I strive to be quick with it."

The following night in Duluth, I recalled the speaker that was still Bluetooth-enabled, and a nurse told me about a guy who had frozen his glass dildo. When he later forced it up his ass, the abrupt temperature change caused it to break, resulting in extensive damage. After cringing, I considered how someone—perhaps me—could introduce the Chilldo, which would be made of Pyrex and so guaranteed not to crack or fracture deep within a user's rectum. I added it to my Million Dollar Idea list, right behind a chain of airport barbershops called O'Hair. Is this why I am not poor? I wondered. Because I am always thinking?

I shared the story about Mary that night as well, and at the end of the evening a woman handed me a fifty-dollar bill and asked that I give it away to someone who needed it.

I decided I'd wait until I reached St. Louis, but near my gate in Minneapolis, where I had a short layover the following afternoon, there was a McDonald's and, walking past it, I observed a woman behind the counter. She was perhaps in her early forties and substantially overweight, with dull gray hair that fell to her jawline. Her spectacles were oval shaped and misaligned. It's weird to give away money. You don't want someone to believe you're pitying them, even if that's what it generally comes down to, and frequently over something so minor—in this case, crooked spectacles. Plus, you'll have to go through airport security every morning just to work at McDonalds.

"Excuse me," I said. "This is going to sound insane, but every day, I choose someone to give $50 to. Do you mind? " I placed the bill on the counter in front of her, wondering if she hadn't misunderstood and believed I said $50,000.

"Oh, goodness! " She yelled like someone on a game show who had just won a huge prize—a boat heaped atop a BMW full of diamonds and the exorbitantly pricey ink cartridges my printer requires at the end of every fifth page. I dashed away, but I could hear her behind me. "Did you see that? Fifty bucks. Oh, my God. Oh, my God. Oh, my God. "

I guess I chose the proper person, I reasoned as I ran to my gate, which was at the far end of the terminal. My flight was delayed for half an hour, and I was hungry. Getting a snack required walking past McDonald's, and I didn't want the woman to see me again, so I sat there and ate three raisins I discovered attached to my checkbook at the bottom of my tote bag. Oh, the cost of saving lives.

I continued to discuss the fifty-dollar bills at my bookstore engagements, expecting that someone might be like the woman in Duluth, but no one came forward, and the subject was eventually overshadowed by the things that males shove up inside themselves. If ladies get home from work and remove their bras, their husbands return and hunt for items to force up their butts. In each city, I was given a different example.

By the time a nurse told me about a patient who had inserted an electric toothbrush inside himself and another who had managed a two-liter bottle of Diet Mountain Dew, I was so used to it that all I could say was, "Wait a minute." Diet? "

It was not my fault that the money theme disappeared. I put stuff out there, and the audience picks what they want to focus on. I believe it was a reflection of the country's mood. Something in the early summer of 2019 made us all think of huge gaping assholes.

My final stop was in Reno. Then I returned to England as if none of this had ever occurred. The only thing that lingered with me was that man in Seattle, the one who would sooner pick crushed cigarette butts off the sidewalk than take the pack I had bought for him, the one who cowered when I approached. During my book tour, I met a lot of people. I shook hands. I asked questions. I connected. I'm not a bad man. So why am I concerned that he was the only person I encountered that month who actually saw me?

CHAPTER 6
HOT DOGS AND HAND SANITIZER

*H*ugh and I live on Manhattan's Upper East Side, and the grocery nearest to our apartment is rarely busy. It does not deserve to be. The place isn't unclean or badly supplied; it's simply sad, thanks in part to the fact that it's mostly subterranean and windowless. Every now and again, they'll recruit a cheery cashier, someone who appears to be getting paid and isn't tethered to the floor under her counter, but the happy ones never last long. I just shop there rarely because it is convenient.

In February 2020, I traveled to South America with my friend Dawn. There had been reports of a virus in China, but I hadn't given it much mind until I traveled from Buenos Aires to Santiago and had my temperature tested while waiting in the Chilean customs line. Well, I thought this was intriguing. It was the first time I'd seen a thermometer shaped like a pistol, and I flinched instinctively as the barrel was placed against my forehead. Is this what I'll do if someone shoots me execution-style? I wondered. Close my eyes and jerk slightly?

On the flight back to New York, I spotted some of my fellow passengers wearing masks and inwardly reprimanded them for overreacting, unaware that by March, my naked bottom would be exposed to more sunlight than the lower half of my face. The grocery shop, which I disliked, was the first hint that things were going apart in the United States. It had gone from zero to sixty customers, practically overnight. Lines abruptly reached the back wall, then snaked back to the registers. Toilet paper was the first to go, followed by the most obvious substitutes: Kleenex, napkins, and paper towels. I remember staring long and hard at the coffee filters, thinking, "Too soon?"

Then there was food for folks who don't cook: prepackaged pizzas and burritos, pasta, jarred spaghetti sauces, and tuna.

There were rumors that booze stores may collapse, resulting in a run on vodka. Not the sort that came in skinny frosted bottles and resembled current dance prizes, but the kind that came in jugs and might have easily had a skull and crossbones on the label.

I tried hoarding. My first try, at a Whole Foods where I had to wait in line, resulted in two steaks and a pouch of dry coconut.

"Coconut? " Hugh said when I arrived home.

I pinched some out like chewing tobacco and stuffed it between my lower gum and cheek. "Well, I've seen you use it for cakes."

That evening, at another neighborhood store, I attempted to hoard again and came home with a pint of buttermilk and some taco shells.

"I give up," Hugh stated.

The following afternoon, I went with my sister Amy to Eataly, a high-end retailer. On that journey, I returned with two sacks of Jordan almonds, an anchovy jar, and a pack of hot dogs.

"You are pathetic! "Hugh said.

"Well, they're not just any hot dogs," I informed him. "These are handcrafted by hot-dog artisans in"—I looked at the label—"New Jersey."

Had I really just used the term "hot-dog artisans?" I asked Amy, "Don't you sometimes despise yourself? "

She was no better at hoarding than I was—an outrage given that we'd both grown up with our father, who was a skilled stockpiler. During the 1973 oil crisis, I recall him going to the Shell station with empty cans and getting in line at four a.m. All of our cars had full tanks, but he need the next guy's ration as well. My sisters and I didn't even know how to drive, but he taught us how to siphon. I vividly recall my first swallow of gasoline, the shock, the wrongness. Spitting it on the street, I thought, "Someone could have used that!"

"Can you imagine Dad 20 years younger? " I stated to Amy after our unsuccessful excursion to Eataly. "If he wasn't locked up in his assisted living facility, he'd have been first in line at his local Sam's Club, loading his forklift with pallets of canned sausages and fruit cocktail." How could we, his children, be so bad at the kind of shopping he took joy in? Have we learned nothing? Lisa, our sister, wasn't doing much better. "Bob and I heard they'd be getting some toilet paper in at Costco, but it was gone by the time we arrived."

"What do you mean with 'by the time we arrived'? "I overheard my father say. "You didn't stay the night outside the front door? You let someone else to take what was rightfully yours. "

One day, I saw hand sanitizer in a small drugstore in my area. There was a sign in the window proclaiming it, and several people stood on the sidewalk, staring at the sign and waiting for someone else to open the door. That happened frequently at first. Nobody wanted to touch the handle. "Fine," I'd always respond, "I'll do it."

Then I'd have to stand there and allow thirty customers pass. Then twenty. Then ten. It was remarkable how rapidly Manhattan deserted. By mid-March, my building was only about a third full, and it got much emptier when it was decided that all work had to be suspended: no more carpenters or decorators. Then no more housekeepers or personal assistants. No more babysitters. No more furniture delivery. Cabs disappeared from the streets. Stores closed or significantly reduced their hours.

Journalists appeared to be the only persons still working. Just when I thought I'd covered every possible facet of the coronavirus, I came upon an article about how it was impacting prostitutes. They couldn't exactly file for unemployment benefits, so several reportedly started GoFundMe campaigns.

When I relayed the article to my agent, Cristina, she responded, "I'm not sure why they can't use Skype. Not that it will actually solve anything. It won't be long before sex robots put all those folks out of business."

Who are you? I wondered. I mean, sexual robots! This was my agent!

There was also FaceTime, which I assumed might be changed in this case to Sit-on-Your-Face Time.

However, many people were relocating their businesses online. Before everything went wrong, Amy had a trainer, a Pilates instructor, and a regular acupuncturist, all of whom advised they continue their sessions electronically.

I said, "The first two make sense, but how does it work with the acupuncturist? Are you supposed to stick the needles into yourself?"

"He said we'd start by looking at my tongue and then talk about my general wellness for an hour," I was told. "I'd like to keep people in business, but this just leaves me feeling overwhelmed."

I had previously volunteered to run errands. If one of my few remaining neighbors had needed something from the grocery store or drugstore, I would have gladly gone to get it. Some individuals suggested that the greatest thing I could do for those around me was to stay indoors. But I could only tolerate so much isolation, and I wasn't getting very close to anyone. When two persons approached each other on the sidewalk, they hugged opposing edges, as if they were enemies. Our eyes didn't even meet anymore.

I'd frequently slog down nineteen levels merely to talk to the doorman. We'd glance out the window at the street, at the traffic that wasn't there, and at the pedestrians who had stopped walking.

"Well, OK, then," I'd remark after about ten minutes. "I guess I'll go see what Hugh is up to."

Then I'd press the elevator button with my elbow and return upstairs, trying hard not to think about sex robots and how much they would cost.

Before the pandemic, I thought my apartment needed to be vacuumed every other day, so after lunch, no matter how busy I was, I'd roll up my sleeves and get to work. Now I knew it had to be done every day—or twice a day if I spent a lot of time at my desk. My workplace chair has an ancient rattan seat that rains down dusty fragments when I sit for too long. These would be tracked from room to room when I refilled my coffee cup or retrieved items from the washing machine, which I'd recently discovered had a specific setting for towels.

Amy remarked, "Get the chair rewoven."

I asked, "By whom?" "

She said, "the blind."

However, the blind were not at their workshops at this time. Who could blame them? Since the shelter-in-place order, I've seen twice as much shit on the streets. I assumed that because there was no one there to yell at dog owners, they didn't bother picking it up. Or they were using the virus as an excuse, acting as if they needed to hurry back indoors immediately once, as if further thirty seconds would result in their death. And who would be stepping in all of this shit? Who are they? The blind!

Still, I volunteered to walk a dog for anyone who was too afraid to go outside. Then I changed it to say I'd be willing to walk any dog with a colostomy bag. I mean, I needed to draw the line someplace.

"What you're doing," Hugh warned me, "is killing time." And he was correct. Vacuuming, cleaning, tormenting my towels with three-hour wash cycles: it was all just busywork until the sun went down and the clock finally struck midnight. Then I'd slip a few dollars into my pocket and sneak outside to a New York I'd never imagined, one in which I was, if not the only person, then at least one of a select few.

Here's a random night out of hundreds: I'd just walked six kilometers and hadn't met anyone. With no traffic to stop me, the only time I'd paused was to read a sign someone had put in the window of a padlocked bar: I USED TO COUGH TO HIDE A FART; NOW I FART TO HIDE A COUGH. I copied the words down in my notebook, then turned a corner to find a man with a black eye and a fistful of potato chips standing in the middle of the sidewalk. "Do you speak English?" He asked.

I learnt years ago not to quit. I know it seems callous, but whether it's a guy with a black eye or a young person with a clipboard, the moment you engage, you're done. I had been with my sister a few months before when a woman holding a cardboard sign asked, "Can I ask you a question?" "

"Aries," Amy called over her shoulder as we raced by.

The man with the black eye told me as I passed that they wouldn't let him on the subway until he had another $1, so I handed it to him, despite the fact that there were no more trains at that time. It was not generosity that prompted me to turn around. I just wanted to have a closer look at his face.

Did you at least fight back? I wanted to ask. The region around his black eye was swollen, and I saw some blood on his clothes.

"I just want to get home, man," he added.

"Me too," I informed him. But in reality, I still had a few miles in me.

Fitbit users, particularly those living under curfews, suffered greatly during the lockdown. I had a pristine step-by-step record and was not going to break it for a raging pandemic.

If I went out after midnight, when the streets were vacant, I couldn't see how I was endangering anyone. The emptiness felt creepy. If I were driving across the city seeking for someone to rob, I would have certainly chosen myself—who wouldn't? I am little. I was always alone and stayed in the shadows like a rat, which I saw a lot of. Some times, there were forty or fifty of them, particularly when the garbage bags were piled high on the curb. They'd flow out as I passed, almost as if on cue, adding to my already overwhelming sense of gloom and societal degradation.

There were other worrisome scenes during the day, such as a couple injecting heroin on Fifth Avenue. They were seated on the ground, their backs against the facade of a business that had barely opened two months earlier and was most likely selling $4,000 crocodile panty shields. When I looked at the two, they returned my gaze with a questioning expression.

Walking home from Amy's place to my own later, I came across a scowling blast furnace of a man who had set up a little encampment beneath a scaffold and surrounded himself with handmade placards, one of which said, FUCK YOU DIAPER FACE.

Normally in New York, one out of every two hundred people you see is insane. It now felt like one in every two. I was at Times Square late one Sunday night. It was deserted, and I came upon a man in a wheelchair who was pushing himself forward with his feet. "Look at this fucking moron! " he yelled.

I looked down at what I was wearing and wondered, "What's wrong with a mechanics jacket that falls to my ankles?"

"Fucking clown!" "The man bayed again. I followed his eyes and spotted a clown with a red nose and turquoise hair standing on the other side of Broadway. Okay, I thought.

My area is well-known for its elderly and wealthy residents, as well as its hospitals. The closest of them now had a refrigerated truck parked outside, storing dead bodies. Sirens sounded around the clock. Looking back, I can't believe I was never sick. Hugh, Amy, and I flew frequently to North Carolina. We'd wave at my father from the window of his locked-down assisted care facility. After a quick coffee stop, we'd head to Emerald Isle, where the coronavirus was widely believed to be a hoax, and unmasked people stared at you in the same way that New York heroin users would, as if to say, Yeah, and what the fuck are you going to do about it?

I wasn't worried about strangers, though. If I had contracted COVID, it would have been from a friend or acquaintance. During the peak of the pandemic, Hugh and I hosted at least two dinner parties per week, and frequently up to four. When questioned, I'd say that the people we invited were part of our bubble. But it was not true. Anyone who wanted to leave their house was welcome. We ate a lot of ground water buffalo in the first several months. That was the one thing I had successfully hoarded. There was a stand selling it in the Union Square farmers' market, and I'd return home once a week with around five pounds' worth.

"What should I cook with this? " Hugh inquired the first time I presented him with it.

I had asked the same inquiry to the vendor. "Use your imagination," he said.

So I told Hugh, "Use your imagination."

We had water buffalo moussaka, water buffalo Bolognese, grape leaves stuffed with water buffalo, and water buffalo enchiladas.

It sounds petty, but if a dinner guest used the word surreal to describe our current position, or the phrase hunkered down, I would make a mental point to exclude them from any future gatherings. I despised the pandemic-related clichés, as well as hearing about the new normal. Ah, and heroes. Originally, the term referred to health-care personnel. Then come the crucial staff. Then, we were all heroes. "Give yourself a big hand, and stay safe!" "

Even more unpleasant was the new spirit of one-upmanship that appeared to have taken hold. A year ago, if I had written in an article, "I woke up and washed my face," no one would have taken it seriously. However, I would be immediately labeled as tone-deaf and elitist.

"Oh, how nice that you can just 'wake up and wash your face,'" someone would say in the comments or on Twitter. "And in New York, no less!" Meanwhile, I've lost my face. I had to sell it to feed my family amid the global pandemic you had apparently never heard of. Now, when I try to eat, the food falls into my lap since I don't have cheeks to keep it in my mouth. Think about that when you're holding your washcloth, you fortunate prick! "

When a formerly popular talk show host began broadcasting from her home, viewers went crazy. "Wait a minute; she lives in a mansion! "

"Well, yes," I intended to say. "A mansion bought with money that you gave her."

Everyone was angry and looking for someone to blame, including Trump, Fauci, China, and Big Pharma. It had to be someone's fault. "Back off! " A particular type of individual would snarl if you were only five feet and eleven inches from them.

"Your mask isn't completely covering your nose," a middle-aged woman told a much older one at my local Target one day. "Miss," she said a moment later to the cashier, "her mask isn't entirely concealing her nose! "

It was a golden age for tattletales, conspiracy theorists, and the self-righteous. A photographer arrived one afternoon to take my picture. I was standing in the middle of East 70th Street posing as directed when a woman with gray hair approached. She was on the sidewalk, about twenty feet away, yet she still felt the need to chastise me. "Cover your face! "She shrieked.

"Oh, for God's sake! This is for the Times! " I yelled back.

I observed a person wearing a T-shirt that said, "DEADLIEST VIRUS IN AMERICA: THE MEDIA."

I saw a woman wearing a T-shirt that said, "You'd look better with a mask on."

"Do you know who I hate? "I told Amy over water buffalo Swedish meatballs that night. "Everyone."

We all jumped at the opportunity to get vaccines. "I'll take whatever you've got and as soon as possible."

In late spring 2021, it was announced that we would no longer be required to wear masks on New York City streets. I lowered my below my nose. The next day, I carried it in my hand and then in my pocket, ready to go whenever I entered a store, my fitness center, or the lobby of my building—anywhere that asked for it. Hugh continued to wear it outside long after it was no longer necessary. When I questioned why, he simply shrugged. "It's just easier."

Over the course of a week, New York returned to itself. Although theaters and symphony venues had not yet reopened, individuals began to return from wherever they had been hiding. There was traffic, and you could easily locate another taxi. As the sidewalks became congested, I thought, Oh no. Now I loathe them much more than I did during the lockdown! How had I forgotten about pedestrians who walk and text at the same time, or dog owners who block your path with their extendable leashes so that their pit bull mix can sniff the ass of someone else's, and both owners can say, with great virtue and often simultaneously, "He's a rescue! "

Neighbors who had decamped to the Hamptons for a year wondered why this or that particular business had gone under.

"Um, because you weren't here to support it? "

Given all the items that disappeared, I was shocked by what survived. I entered a long-closed store one afternoon seeking for a gift for Hugh's nephew, and the clerk remarked, "Welcome in."

"Really? "I said. "That endured—'Welcome in'? " I'd hoped it might have been forgotten, or consigned to the past like "Howdy-do." I can't stand "Welcome in."

"You don't need the in part," I've said to salesclerks more times than I can count. Then I become the weirdo who's correcting folks about their grammar.

The terrible shame about the pandemic in the United States is that more than nine hundred thousand people have died to date, and I didn't get to choose a one of them. It's unfair that we lost Terrence McNally but not the guy on the electric scooter who nearly hit me on Seventh Avenue one warm day in summer 2021. As I turned to chastise him, he collided with a woman on a bicycle who had rushed past a red light while gazing down at her phone. Both of them crashed down the street, the sound of screeching brakes all around them, and I remembered, the way you might recollect a pleasant dream you'd once had, that things aren't as horrible as they often appear, and life can truly be lovely.

CHAPTER 7
HOW DO WE GET TO THE OTHER SIDE?

When George Floyd was assassinated and New York suddenly smelled like fresh plywood, I thought of Schenectady.

"Why there?" my sister Amy inquired. She was with Hugh and me on the patio of our Upper East Side apartment in Manhattan. From where we stood, we could hear the churning cauldron twenty stories below us: sirens, shouting, and distant sounds of breaking glass—all combined into a violent, muted roar.

"Years ago I was on a plane, seated next to a middle-aged Black woman who was reading a Bible," I told her. "I was doing a crossword puzzle and asked the flight attendant—a white male, not just homosexual but a queen—'Excuse me, but do you know how to spell Schenectady?'

"He told me that he had no idea, and just as I was sort of hating him for it, the woman with the Bible said, 'S-c-h-e-n-e-c-t-a-d-y.' She spelled it with her eyes shut, maybe to prove that she wasn't cheating."

Amy spat an olive pit in her palm. "Oops."

"Exactly," I replied. "Why hadn't I turned to her first?" I told myself I asked the flight attendant since it was his job to serve me, but was that really true? Did I question him because he was white or because he wasn't reading his Bible?"

What does that have to do with anything? "Amy inquired.

I shrugged. "I guess I don't think that people who read Bibles on planes are all that smart."

"I don't know that being smart really plays into it," she remarked. "I'm sure there are plenty of dummies in Schenectady who have no trouble spelling their hometown's name. I mean, it's part of their address." She placed the olive pit in a planter Hugh had just filled with pansies. "I cannot spell Minneapolis or Minnesota. Does this make me stupid? "

I answered, "Yes."

She exhaled. "I understand. "I am an idiot."

Hugh went indoors to prepare new drinks for himself and Amy. "I could have spelled Schenectady for you."

"Yes, but you weren't there, were you?" "I said. "You're never there when I really need you."

He and I had recently returned from two weeks in the Sea Section. COVID-19 had already changed the New York we'd left behind, but now that we'd returned, it felt even more different. For the first time since February, the virus was not the only story; the unrest was. The country had gone from one massive headline story to the next, and it seemed like anything could happen next: a catastrophic natural disaster, an alien invasion. If I was overreacting, it was because New York had been hit harder by the year 2020 than many other places, such as North Carolina.

"The coronavirus never happened on Emerald Isle," I told my wife. "Okay, it almost didn't happen. At the grocery store, almost no one was wearing a mask. Likewise at Dairy Queen. Coming from Manhattan, where we can't leave the house without our faces covered, it was a real…" I'd planned to say shock, but instead came out with vacation.

"I want to go," Amy stated. So we planned to return in a few weeks with her and her friend Adam. Meanwhile, shops were looted, and there were almost constant local protests, ranging from peaceful to confrontational. Five months before, I'd been in Hong Kong and questioned people about the pro-democracy demonstrations, only to discover that if you lived in certain parts of town and ignored television, you could easily be unaware of them. That was not the situation in New York, where protests were impossible to ignore regardless of area.

I walked downtown the day after Amy arrived for supper and stumbled into a crowd gathered in Union Square. A number of individuals had placards, but before I could read them, I was stopped by a young woman with green hair who offered me a plastic bottle.

"Water, sir? "

I shook my head no.

"How about some hand sanitizer? Or I have chips if you need a little something to eat." I guessed that she was a college student and assumed she was selling these things. But no, it seemed they were free.

"That's all right, but thanks," I said.

The gathering near the southern edge of the park wasn't doing anything in particular. Some of the people who had placards were hoisting them with no apparent sense of urgency in the direction of the police, who formed a ragged line on the other side of 14th Street, conversing among themselves. Protest-wise, it seemed a nice location to get started, so I went to Amy's and returned with her half an hour later, commenting as we waded into the throng, "We look like we're searching for our children."

Grandchildren was probably more like it, as we were by far the oldest persons I saw.

"Water? " an earnest woman with pigtails asked. "Do you want any pretzels? Anything to raise your blood sugar? "

"Need a list of all the neighborhood restrooms? " another student-aged person inquired, handing me a clearly defined map. This was not what the television news had shown. There were no crowbars, only candy bars. Also chips, Cheetos, and dried fruit slices. "Are you certain I can't give you something to eat? " questioned a determined young snacktivist.

I estimated there were about three hundred individuals in the park. Signs read WHITE SILENCE NO MORE, DEFUND NYPD, NO EXCUSE 4 ABUSE, and BLM, which stands for Black Lives Matter. Someone I couldn't see was beating a drum, and while it seemed like something should happen, nothing happened. Applause would occasionally break out, but I had no idea why.

"It's just a gathering," the young woman standing next to me said. She had a ring on her nose and, like most of the people around us, was white.

The alley is a weird place to be. On another website that morning, I saw a video of two identical-looking blondes spray-painting I CAN'T BREATHE on the front of a Starbucks in Los Angeles.

"What are you doing?" " a Black demonstrator exclaimed. "That's something I'm going to get blamed for. My people. Who asked for your assistance, anyway? "

The females stopped only because they were done. In another video, a white man with silver hair was breaking up paving stones to throw at the cops with a pick, similar to the ones used by gold miners in movies.

A Black protester intervened, saying something similar to the woman in Los Angeles. He knew he would be blamed for it. But the person with the pick persisted until he was brought to the ground by the Black fellow and a handful of his buddies, who then delivered him to the officers he planned to stone.

I planned to assist the movement in the same way I had previously done: by donating money and then informing everyone I had donated twice as much. When I sent in my contributions, I regarded the protests differently; now I had done something and could feel superior to those who hadn't.

Looting occurred during the early days of the protests, and the press coverage made me concerned. My fear was that my favorite stores would be vacated, and that when the city reopened following the COVID limitations, there would be nothing left for me to buy. Amy shared my anxiety, so we left Union Square and walked to SoHo, which included two of our favorite businesses. Both were boarded up, but I wasn't sure if it was a precaution or the result of broken windows.

"It's not like I really need anything," I grumbled as we returned uptown. We'd never gone this long without shopping—nearly a hundred days—and I wasn't sure who I was anymore. When my agent's birthday arrived, I gave her two bottles of wine and a gift card to a pharmacy she like. "Those are, like, presents Lisa would come up with," I told Amy. Our sister is not inherently cheap; rather, she is unimaginative.

There were so many questions I needed answered. How, for example, did people find the shoe style they wanted, let alone the correct size, while robbing large Nike stores? "You're an amateur wandering around a massive, probably dark stockroom with ten minutes at most, while the salesclerks, who are pros, seem to need twice that amount of time," I told her.

We just happened to come across a protest march that was actually moving. It was coming our way, west on Houston Street, so we followed it. Again, it was difficult to assess the crowd number. One thousand people? More? Social separation was in effect, and almost everyone I encountered had the lower half of their faces covered. In this occasion, I actually appreciated my mask since it removed some of the pressure of chanting, which I've never been comfortable with. The same goes for prayer and the Pledge of Allegiance. I even lip-synced "Happy Birthday," so I was relieved that my mouth was concealed and no one could tell if I was participating.

"Hey, hey / Ho, ho / Racist cops need to go! "The throng yelled as Amy and I merged into it. This template, which has been around since the 1950s, is by far my least favorite. True, it can be easily customized to any purpose, but you always know what word will rhyme with ho: go. It's lazy.

Then came "Whose streets?" "

"Our streets!" "

Then it was: "NYPD, suck my dick."

I am not sure how I feel about that. Is fellatio the most severe punishment you can imagine? I wanted to ask. I was thinking they'd modify it to "NYPD, kiss my ass," but that has its uses as well. "Eat me out" ? "Drink my piss" ? Anything sexual is likely to offend someone.

"Black lives matter!" " followed by "Suck my dick!" " and then we were back to "Whose streets? Our streets! "It's always fascinating to watch a chant dwindle, like a match ending. Some people can burn for long periods of time, but this throng seemed to follow a rigorous forty-five-second rule.

Everyone seemed to have their phones out, and I saw a number of individuals shooting selfies. This struck me as obscene, but what isn't a backdrop for an Instagram image nowadays? When searching for "selfies at…," "…funerals" came up as the third option on Google. I clicked on it, shocked to see mourners posing near the caskets of their deceased friends and family. Some people raised their thumbs, but what precisely did this mean? Great embalming job? Great death?

The march went west before turning north onto LaGuardia Place. It became congested at Washington Square Park, so Amy and I decided to leave. I walked her home before continuing on foot to my apartment, which was another fifty-three streets north.

As time passed and the marches got more common, I began to think about them in the same way that I do buses and subways. I'll just take the BLM down to 23rd Street. The people were polite, the snacks plentiful, and it felt good to walk down the middle of the avenue.

At 23rd, I might wait an hour or more before taking another BLM back home or across town to the West Side. While marching, I would look about and wonder what everyone else was thinking. It's like being at the symphony. I always imagined that the audience was comparing this performance of, say, Mahler's Second Symphony to a superior one. Then I began asking around and discovered that others were having the same strange thoughts as I was: how long would it take me to eat all of my clothes—not the zippers and buttons, but just the fabric? Could I do it in six months? Would your body notice if you finely shredded a sport coat and mixed half a cup into, say, stuffing?

While marching, I was confident that everyone around me was thinking about racism and the countless Black Americans killed by police officers throughout the years. We white people probably contemplated our own culpability, or at least touched on it briefly—that exposed wire—before going on to other individuals who were far worse than us. But as time passed, our thoughts strayed, didn't they?

One afternoon, while I marched uptown with a large crowd, I remembered a well-known movie actor who had approached me over thirty years before, when Hugh and I lived in SoHo. He invited me to his residence to explore a potential partnership, and I was flattered because I had never met anyone famous. It was snowing, and over three feet had accumulated by the time I left my apartment. The actor didn't live far from me, maybe a half-mile away, but getting there was difficult due to my short legs and the lack of waterproof boots.

When I arrived, his two young children—a boy and a girl—were in the dining room, being served by a thin Black woman with a do-rag over her hair. She waved hello to me as we passed by, and I noticed the steam rising from the soup she was setting down.

"You're lucky she came into work in this weather," I told the actor as we made our way to the living room. "On a Saturday, no less!" "

He gave a faint smile. "Actually, that's my wife."

My cheek still hurts just thinking about it, but at the very least, it taught me something. From that day forward, anytime I visit someone's house and see a person of a different race working inside or outdoors, I ask, "Is that your husband? " or "Why do you make your wife do all the cleaning?" "

They invariably respond, "Conchita, my wife?" She's around twenty years older than me and has four children. Plus, I'm already married. To a man." Eventually, though, I'll be right, and my host will say, "May I just thank you for being the only person in my life who isn't a disgusting racist? "

As the weeks passed, I saw more and more protest signs reading DEFUND THE POLICE, which will not do us much good come election time, I thought, worried about how this would play on Fox News: "The left wants it so that when armed thugs break into your house and you dial 911, you'll get a recording of Rich Homie Quan laughing at you!" "

Amy worried too. It wasn't cutting money earmarked for law enforcement and putting it toward social services that troubled her—rather, it was the terminology and how Trump would use it to intimidate people. He'd already begun, and I expected him to keep working on it until the election.

"Then there are all the statues being pulled down," Amy stated when she and Adam landed on Emerald Isle. "I'd thought that would be nearly impossible, that they were, like, screwed into the ground or something, but I guess all you need is some good rope and a dozen or so really mad people."

"Mad strong people," Adam said.

"I'm not sure the general public really pays all that much attention to statues," I claimed. "Don't you think you could come in the middle of the night and replace General Braxton Bragg's head with that of, say, Whoopi Goldberg, and no one would notice for months? Don't most of us think of a bronze figure on a pedestal as just a statue? "

Amy guessed that I was correct.

"For those few exceptions who pay closer attention, you could keep the monument and change the plaque," I suggested. "It could read something like CHESTER BEAUREGARD JR.—UNFORTUNATE BLACKSMITH WHO BORE A STRIKING RESEMBLANCE TO THE TRAITOR GENERAL BRAXTON BRAGG."

When I brought up the topic over the phone the next day with my Jewish friend Asya, she disagreed. "If there were statues of famous Nazis around, even ones with replaced heads and nameplates, I still wouldn't want to pass them every day," she told me. "Ugh, what a slap in the face!" "

I get her point. To individuals who are concerned over the recently toppled monuments, I suppose I would say, "Look, times change. For a hundred years, Jefferson Davis ignored your pitiful traffic circle. Now we'll just put him in storage and give someone else a turn for a bit."

"Who would argue with that? I asked my friends John and Lynette, who live near the Sea Section. I believed the streets in our community were named after the developer's children, but it appears I was mistaken. "That's Lee Avenue, as in Robert E.," John explained. "Stuart Avenue as in Jeb, and Jackson as in Stonewall."

When I repeated this to Amy, she said, "What about Scotch Bonnet Drive? "

"That's after, um, General Jedediah Scotch Bonnet," I told the woman.

There was also a street called Coon Crossing. A year ago, I would have dismissed it, but now I was reconsidering everything. I was shocked to learn that John and Lynette's Raleigh neighborhood, Cameron Village, was now just known as the Village District, owing to the fact that the Cameron it was named after was a plantation owner. This made me ponder about the men who run my primary and high schools. Who was E? C. Brooks? Jesse Sanderson?

Meanwhile, Uncle Ben's rice became known as Ben's Original. The box remained orange, but the face was no longer visible. Eskimo Pies vanished as well.

"I was fine with all this Black Lives Matter stuff until they went after both Aunt Jemima and Mrs. Butterworth's," stated Bermey, one of our friends. "Now I'm saying, 'Hey, don't fuck with my syrup! '"

A Confederate flag beach towel was displayed in the window of one of the island's many businesses selling inflatable rafts and affordable apparel. I spotted quite a few of these in eastern North Carolina. Some were subtle (a decal on a windshield), but others were loud: full-sized standards blowing in front of residences, frequently beside a TRUMP flag, or fastened to large pickup trucks that would tear up and down the main road. The vehicles were unusually high off the ground, with jacked-up front wheels that made them appear to be constantly climbing uphill—Carolina Squats, or bro dozers. Their mufflers had also been modified, or perhaps they were completely removed. The engines roared, as if to proclaim, "Asshole coming through!" " If there was any doubt that the driver was worried about his masculinity, a pair of lemon-sized testicles might frequently be found dangling from the trailer hitch.

"Lord, son," Bermey said, surprised as I recounted them to him. "Have you never seen Truck Nutz?"

I was eight years old when we moved south from New York. It was the first time I'd heard the words Yankee and Rebel. In school, Cub Scouts, and the country club, you were either on one side or another. Those that win the conflict move on. People who lose use their flags as beach towels and hang firm rubber testicles from their bumpers. They make it convenient for the rest of us to conceal. "Over there!" "We say, pointing to a bro dozer with a Confederate flag on it. "That's what a racist looks like."

When I was in seventh school, I served as the campaign manager for Dwight Bunch, one of Carroll Junior High's three Black students. He ran for class president—and won—using my wonderful slogan "We Like Dwight a Bunch." Two years later, our school was desegregated. Fights broke out in the parking lot. My pal Ted's nose was broken with a Coke bottle. In our twenties, we both dated a number of Black men, which I always thought made us the antithesis of bigots. I didn't have sex with them because of their race, but because they were present and eager. Now I was reading that sleeping with Black men meant you were prejudiced and exoticized them.

Everything was suspicious, and everywhere you looked, there was an article labeled "_____'s Race Problem."

It might be about anyone: an actor who has never worked with a person of race, or a comedian who used the term "Negro" twenty years ago. The pieces were consistently written by white folks in their early twenties.

I spotted the word POC (White Passing) in someone's email signature and wondered how long it had been in use.

Reckoning was a word I kept hearing. It was time for a race reckoning.

We spent two weeks at the beach and returned to New York just as the protests had subsided into bike-riding chances. Flash mobs of mostly white people would ride up the avenues, three thousand strong, halting traffic and yelling, "Whose streets?" Our streets!" and, occasionally, "Black Lives Matter! "—but weirdly, in the singsongy way a fishmonger might call, "Fresh-caught haddock!"

I stumbled onto a bike march one Saturday afternoon, the last day of spring, about five o'clock. People lined Third Avenue, with the majority raising their phones to capture pictures and videos or to turn away from the bicycles and take selfies. Beside me stood two white girls in their early twenties, each texting furiously.

"How can I get across? " inquired a frail-looking old woman who had suddenly materialized next me. Her rust-colored wig was pushed low across her forehead, and she wore a sun visor. She was holding a large bag from a local drugstore.

"You wait until these people are done," said one of the tanned girls.

I, who, of course, wanted to urinate, was asking the same question: how could I cross? How do I, and all of us, get to the other side?

CHAPTER 8
KING OF CLUTTER, PRINCE OF TURTLES

*S*omething about a car running over a cop and injuring another officer. This is my opinion of a news item that aired on the television in my father's room at Springmoor, where he has been residing for the past three years. It is early April, three days before his ninety-eighth birthday, and Amy, Hugh, and I have just flown to Raleigh from New York. The goal is to hang out for a while before driving to our home on Emerald Isle.

Dad is in his wheelchair, clothed and ready for our visit. Hair combed. He wears real shoes. A red bandanna hung around his neck. "Well, hello!" he calls as we walk in, an old turtle raising his head to the sun. "It's great to see you, kids!"

Hugh wonders if we may turn off the television as Amy and I go in to embrace him.

"Well, sure," my father, still surrounded by adult children, responds. "I don't even know why it's on, to tell you the truth."

Hugh removes the remote from the bedside table, and after he destroys the television, Amy asks if he can fix the radio. As a non-blood relative, he appears to be the servant during our travels to Springmoor.

"Find us a jazz station," I instruct him.

"Here we go!" My father says. "That'd be amazing!"

Amy and I no longer care about the news, particularly political news. I'm faintly aware that Andrew Cuomo has fallen out of favor, and that people other than me will be receiving government payments for various reasons, but that's about it. When Trump was president, I began each morning by reading the New York Times, followed by the Washington Post, and checked both papers' websites throughout the day. Being less than watchful meant falling behind, and what could be worse than not knowing what Stephen Miller had just stated about Wisconsin? My friend Mike likened the constant monitoring to working a second job. It was taxing, and the instant Biden was sworn into office, I let it all go. When the new president speaks, I feel the same feeling I do on a plane when the captain declares that after reaching our cruising altitude, we will head directly north or turn left at Lake Erie. You don't have to inform me about your job, I always think. Just do it.

It's incredibly liberating to no longer listen to political podcasts and feel furious. I continue to read the dailies, avoiding the COVID articles because I am also done with them. The moment I received my first dose of the vaccination, I began to think about the coronavirus in the same way that I think of scurvy—something from a distant past that can no longer harm me, something that mostly affects pirates. "Yes," the journals would reply, "but what if there is a strong surge this summer? What about this Christmas? One year from now? What if the next epidemic is worse than the current one? What if it kills all of the fish, livestock, and poultry and alters our skin's response to sunlight? What if everyone is forced to live below and survive on earthworms?"

My father tested positive for coronavirus shortly before Christmas, around the time he began wheeling himself to Springmoor's front desk and inquiring whether anybody had seen his mother. He doesn't have Alzheimer's, or something as bad. Rather, he is what was once referred to as "soft in the head." Gaga. It's a recent development; except from the moment he was discovered on the floor of his home, dehydrated and suffering from a bladder infection, he's always been not only coherent but authoritative.

"If it happens several times in a day, someone on the staff will contact me," Lisa explained over the phone. "Then I'll call and say, 'Dad, your mother died in 1976 and is buried with your father at the Rural Cemetery in Cortland, New York. You purchased the plot adjacent to theirs, therefore that is where you will be going.

There had to be a softer way to say it, but I'm not sure the news really hit home, especially after his diagnosis, when he was at his lowest. Every time the phone rang, I expected to hear about his death. But my father recovered. "Without being hospitalized," I informed my cousin Nancy. "And he lost ten pounds! " Not that he had to.

When I ask him what it was like to have the coronavirus, he laughs unconvincingly. He says "Ha ha!" a lot now. " I suspect it's a cover for his failed hearing, rather than saying, "Could you repeat that? ," he assumes you're telling a joke of some sort. "Hugh and I just went to Louisville to see his mother," I told my father the last time we visited Springmoor. "Joan is ninety now and has blood cancer."

"Ha ha! "

That was during Halloween. My father's building's outdoor courtyard allowed socially distant visits, and after our allocated thirty minutes, an aide disguised as a witch carried him back to his room.

"The costumes must have done a real number on some of the residents," Amy said as we walked with Hugh to our rental vehicle. "Then a vampire came to take my blood pressure!" '

"'Sure he did, Grandpa.'"

All visits were canceled a few days later, and Springmoor was locked down. Except for the staff, no one is allowed in or out, and all inhabitants are confined to their rooms. The policy was not reversed until six months later. We flew down from New York to see him.

"You look great, Dad," Amy exclaims, almost but not quite shouting. Hugh has finally located a jazz station and has successfully tuned out the static.

"Well, I'm one hundred years old! "My father tells us." "Can you beat that?" "

"Ninety-eight," Amy corrects him. "And not just yet. Your birthday falls on Monday, and today is only Friday."

"One hundred years old!" "

This is not a case of softheadedness, but rather a lifelong predisposition to exaggerate. "What the hell are you still up to?" " he'd demand of my brother, my sisters, and me every school night of our lives. It's one o'clock in the morning! "

We'd point to the nearest clock. "Actually it's nine forty-five."

"It's one o'clock! Dammit! "

"So how come Barnaby Jones is still on? "

"Go to bed!" "

Amy has brought my father some chocolate turtles, and as he watches, she opens the box and gives him one. "Your room also looks good. It's clean, and your belongings fit in nicely."

"It isn't bad, right? "My father says. "You might not believe it, but this is the exact same square footage as the house—the basement of it, anyway."

This is simply false, yet we let it go.

"There are a few things I'd like to get rid of, but overall it's not too cluttered," he says, shifting jerkily in his wheelchair. "That used to be a big issue for me. "I used to be the King of Clutter."

If I were his decorator, I would absolutely remove the Christmas tree that is collecting dust on the console beneath his TV. It's a foot and a half tall and made of plastic. It may look fine when naked, but its decorations, which are the size of juniper berries and flashy, depress me. Next to it is a stack of cards from folks I don't know or whose names I just vaguely recognize from the Greek Orthodox Church. "Has the priest stopped by?" " I ask.

My father nods. "Several times. He doesn't particularly like me, though."

Amy takes a seat on the bed. "Why not?" "

He laughs. "Let me just state that I am not as generous as I could be! "

My father seems slimmer than the last time I saw him, but nevertheless his face is bigger. Something else is different as well, but I can't place my finger on it. It's similar to how superstars get stuff done. I can see they've changed, but I can't tell what it is. The eyes? What about the mouth? I will ponder while looking at a snapshot on a gossip website. "You don't look the same for some reason," I explain to my father.

He looks from me to Hugh, then Amy. "So, you do. All of you do. The only person who has changed is me. I'm one hundred years old! "

"Ninety-eight on Monday," Amy says.

"One hundred years old!" "

"Have you had your COVID vaccine? " I ask, knowing he has.

"I'm not sure," he admits. "Maybe."

I take up a salmon cut from something hard and porous, possibly an antler. It used to be in his basement office at home. This was before he converted every room into an office and immersed himself in envelopes. "Hugh and me and Amy, we've each had one shot."

My dad laughs. "Well, good on you. I haven't taken a drink since I arrived here."

At first, I thought this was a non sequitur, but then I realized he misunderstood what we meant by "shot."

"They don't allow you to drink? " I ask.

"You may have a bit, I suppose, but it's not easy. You have to order it in advance, like medicine, and you only receive a thimbleful," he says in hushed tones.

"Imagine you had a screwdriver. What would happen? Amy asks.

He considers for a moment. "I'd probably get an erection! "

I truly enjoy the new version of my father. He's personable, optimistic, and full of surprises. "One of the things I like about us as a family is that we laugh," he said. "Always! As long back as I can recall. This is what we're known for! "

The majority of the laughter was directed at him, and it began as soon as he exited the room where the rest of us were. He was clearly not a Merriment Club member. But I enjoy how he remembers things differently. "My offbeat sense of humor has won me a lot of friends," he says. "A hell of a lot."

"Are there any friends here?" Amy asks.

"All over the damn place!" Even the youngsters I used to roller-skate with stop by occasionally."

He opens his palm, revealing that the chocolate turtle he was holding had melted. Amy grabs some toilet paper from the bathroom, and he sits calmly while she cleans him up. "What are you wearing?" He asks.

She takes a step back to show him her black-and-white polka-dot shift. Over it, a Japanese denim shirt with coaster-sized smiley-face patches runs up and down the sleeves. Her buddy Paul just informed her that she dresses like a fat person, the stubborn type who thinks, Do you want to laugh? I'll give you something to chuckle about.

"Interesting," my father responds.

Whenever the talk slows, dad returns to one of several topics, the first of which is the inexpensive guitar he purchased me as a youngster and insisted on bringing with him to Springmoor—despite the fact that it had been forgotten in a closet for more than half a century. "I'm trying to teach myself to play, but I just can't find the time to practice."

It appears to me that all he has is time. What else is there to do here but shut up in his room? "I need to make some music!" " he says. As he shakes his fist in disgust, I realize he still has chocolate under his fingernails.

"You're too hard on yourself, Dad," Amy says him. "You don't have to do everything, you understand. Maybe it's okay to simply rest for a change."

His second favorite topic is the artwork on his walls, the most of which dad and my mother purchased in the 1970s and early 1980s. "Now this," he says, pointing to a framed serigraph over his bed, "this I could look at every minute of the day." It is a sentimental, naïf-style street scene of Paris in the early twentieth century—a veritable checklist of tropes and clichés by Michel Delacroix, who defines himself as a "painter of dreams and of the poetic past." On the two occasions when my father visited me in the actual Paris, he couldn't leave fast enough. He can just stand in pictures. "I've got to write this guy a letter and tell him what his work means to me," he said. "The trick is to find the damn time!" "

Two of the paintings in the room were done by my father in the late 1960s. His artistic period came out of nowhere, and he was prolific during its brief six-month run, producing twenty or so canvases, the majority of which were painted with a palette knife rather than a brush. All of them are replicas of van Gogh, Zurbarán, and Picasso. They wouldn't fool anyone, but as children, we were blown away by his brilliance. The challenge was deciding what to paint, or, in his case, copy. Some of his choices were questionable—a stagecoach silhouetted against a tangerine-colored sunset comes to mind—but in reflection, they blended seamlessly with the rest of the house. Back in the 1970s, we considered our color palette to be permanently current. What could possibly replace all that orange, brown, and avocado? It was hilarious in the early 1980s, but now it's back, and we can remember our milk-chocolate walls, the big wicker burro that used to pout atop the piano, and one of our father's acrylic bullfighters presumably afire on the wall behind it.

When Dad retired from IBM, his artwork became a bigger part of his identity. He had been an engineer, but he was also an art enthusiast. This did not include museums; who needed them when he had his living room! "I'm an actual collector, while David, he's more of an investor," he sniffed to my friend Lee after I purchased a Picasso that was painted by Picasso and did not resemble—dare I say it—cake icing.

Then there's my father's mask collection, some of which hang high on the wall above his bed. The best of them were manufactured by tribes in the Pacific Northwest and Alaska and purchased during fly-fishing trips. Several others are African or Mexican. They used to stare down from the paneled wall above the stairs in our house, and it's strange but not unpleasant to see them in this new environment. When I walk down the hall at Springmoor, I always look into the other rooms, none of which are like my father's. There are the neighbors, and then there's Dad—Dad, who's listening to Eric Dolphy while holding a guitar he's never played before. "You know, four of the strings on this thing come from my old violin, which I had in grade school! "

No, they didn't, and who cares? Before his mind began to go, my father consumed a regular diet of Fox News and conservative talk radio, which kept him on edge at all times. "Who is that black guy?" "He demanded in 2014. The family was gathering at the Sea Section, and we were discussing about Michael Brown, who had been shot and killed three months before in Ferguson, Missouri.

"Which Black guy? "I asked.

"Oh, you know the one."

"Bill Cosby?" "Amy offered.

"Gil Scott-Heron?" "I asked.

"Stevie Wonder?" "Gretchen called from the living room.

Lisa asked, "Denzel Washington?" "

"You know who I mean," Dad said. "He's got that son."

"Jesse Jackson?" "

"He is the one. "Always causing trouble."

Now, however, our father has taken a few steps back and, like me, appears to be better for it. "How did you feel when Joe Biden was elected? " I ask. The question violates the bargain Amy and I made before we arrived: don't rile him up or confuse him.

"Actually," the man replies, "I was for that other one."

Hugh says "Trump."

My dad nods. "That's correct. I believed what he told us. And, well, it appears that I was mistaken. "That guy was bad news."

I never expected to hear this: Trump was "bad" and "I was wrong" in the same sentence. "Who are you?" I want to question the lovely gnome in front of me, "What have you done with Lou Sedaris? "

"So, Biden...I guess he's OK," my father replies, wearing his red bandanna like a socialist he never was.

Amy, Hugh, and I are just recovering when an aide enters and announces that it is five o'clock, time for dinner. "I'll wheel Mr. Sedaris down..."

"Oh, we'll take him," Amy replies.

"Take what? " my father inquires, perplexed by the unusual activity.

I shove him out the door and past a television that is showing the news. Again, the incident at the Capitol. Some people were hit by cars, and one person was shot.

"This is like that old joke," I tell my father as we approach the dining room. "A man complains to his wife, 'You're always dragging me around and talking behind my back.' She responds, 'What do you expect—you're in a wheelchair!'"

My father exclaims, "Ha!" "

When we arrive, the dining room, which can seat approximately six tables, is already filled. Women outweigh men, and only we and the staff are ambulatory. The air should smell like food, but it actually smells like Amy's perfume. She wears so much that it both precedes and follows her, staying long after she has left. That said, I enjoy it. It's a blend of five various scents, none of which are flowery or particularly pleasant, and it leaves her smelling like an odd cookie, possibly one with pencil shavings.

"Why don't you eat?" "My father says.

I am aware that everyone is watching. Visitors! Lou has guests!

While Amy and Hugh converse with an attendant, my father looks up and pats the table near him. "Stay for dinner." "They can make you whatever you want."

I can't recall my mother's final words to me. They were presented over phone at the end of a casual talk. "See you," she might have said, or "I'll call back in a few days."

And, in the careless way you do when you believe you have forever with the person on the other end of the line, I most likely said, "OK."

My father's final words to me, said in the too-hot, too-bright dining room of his assisted living home three days before his ninety-eighth birthday, were "Don't go yet. "Do not leave."

My final words to him—and I believe they are as telling as his, given everything we've been through—are "We need to get to the beach before the grocery stores close." They appear cold on paper, and when he dies a few weeks later and I realize they are the last words I said to him, I will think, Maybe I can warm them up onstage when I read this part out loud. Instead of worrying about his death, I'll be thinking about the tale of his death, to the point where Amy will question, "Did I see you taking notes during the service?" "

Her voice will be unsurprising. Rather, it will be the way you might playfully chastise a squirrel: "Did you just jump up from the deck and completely empty that bird feeder?" "

The squirrel and I have a natural affinity, however it may not last forever. My father recently taught me that our natures may alter. Or perhaps they're simply revealed, and the sweet, cheery man I saw that afternoon at Springmoor was always there, buried beneath layers of fury and impatience that burnt away as he blazed into the homestretch.

For the time being, however, as I leave the dining room with Hugh and Amy, I'm thinking that we'll have to do this again, and soon. Fly to Raleigh. See Dad. Perhaps have a picnic in his room. I'll convince Gretchen into coming. Lisa will also be there, as will our brother, Paul.

We'll all be laughing so hard that some assistant will beg us to close the door. Because isn't that what we're known for?

CHAPTER 9
HE DIED, NOT PASSED

*I*sn't it all of our finest work about death—its brutality and inevitability? The shadow it casts over our all-too-brief lives? "What does it all mean?" "We ask ourselves.

Allow me to explain: Death implies that the dinner reservation you booked for a party of seven must be raised to 10, then reduced to nine, and then raised again, this time to fourteen. Eighteen will eventually arrive, so you'll have to sit at a four-top on the opposite side of the room with people you barely recognize, listening as the fun table, which includes your shining sister, laughs and laughs. Meanwhile, you have to hear comments like, "Well, I know that your father did his best."

People enjoy saying this after a parent dies. It's the first item kids reach for. A man can beat his wife with car antennae and trade his children for drugs or motorcycles, but when he finally, thankfully, dies, his survivors will have to hear from some know-nothing at the post-funeral supper that he tried his hardest. This, I believe, is based on the notion that we all give our all in everything: our employment, our relationships, the attention we devote to our appearance, and so on.

"Look around," I'd like to say. "Very few people are doing their best. This is why they get sacked from their employment. This is why they are arrested and divorced. This is why their teeth fall out. Do you believe the 'cook' in charge of this soggy spanakopita is doing his best? Is sitting across from me and uttering clichés and platitudes really the best you can do? "

Also, don't use the word passed at this table unless it's something like, "Tula passed me the salt so I could flavor my tasteless tzatziki sauce," or "I knew we were driving too slowly on our way to the funeral when the hearse passed us and the man driving it gave me the finger."

My father did not die. Neither did he leave. He died.

Why use euphemisms? Who do they help? I remember hearing a woman on the radio a few years ago commenting on where she was when Prince, the artist, "transitioned."

Really? I thought. When exactly did he become a woman? Days before his fatal overdose?

Also, can we put the whole looking down from heaven thing to rest? This means the following: "I'm sure your mother is looking down right now at you and your family…"

Are you sure about that? Sure, there's a heaven right above the cloud cover, one that no satellite or spacecraft has ever detected, and my long-dead mother can peer down from it and see my brother, sisters, and me indoors, some of us wearing hats, among the roughly eight billion other people on Earth, and without her glasses, because they weren't with her in the box she was burned to ashes in. Because if that were feasible, she wouldn't be thinking, "I'm so proud of my son, but why is he listening to that asshole?"

If anything, my father is staring up at me rather than down. He was ninety-eight—"A blessing," you often remark. "He must have been a wonderful man to have been rewarded with such a long life." As if it worked like that, with additional years added for good behavior. Many decent people die at a young age. Do you know someone lives a "good long life"? Dick Cheney. Henry Kissinger. Rupert Murdoch.

"He'll always be with you" is another tired chestnut that I'd prefer never to hear again. In response, I ask, "What if I don't want him with me? "What if sixty-four years of relentless criticism and belittlement were enough, and I'm perfectly comfortable with my father and I parting ways, him in a cooler at the funeral home and me here at the kids' table? He won't be in his grave for a few days. Is that the "better place" you've been telling me he's going to, the cemetery we pass on the way to the airport? The site has a view of the Roy Rogers parking lot. And what exactly is it superior to? This restaurant, obviously, but what else? What is the current state? This country? This earth?

No offense, but how are you so certain of his whereabouts? You had no idea where the men's room was until I told you, so why should I suddenly assume you're omniscient? The best you can say with any degree of certainty is that my father is somewhere else, which means that it is not the only restaurant in town that can accommodate a party of eighteen with five hours' notice, which it can only do because no one else wants to eat here, especially me—it's just that I need to keep my strength up. Because I am grieving.

One night, when I was about ten or eleven years old, I whined at the dinner table about my stomach pains. It hadn't prevented me from cleaning my plate, so I probably mentioned it in an attempt to get out of school the next day. My goal was to fabricate a symptom at six p.m., add a headache before bedtime, and possibly toss in some reported diarrhea in the morning. I just wanted a small break from the fifth grade, I think.

"Let's see how you feel later on," my mother said. "Maybe there's something going around."

I was at my desk shortly after, combing my guinea pig, when my father came in. It was always strange having him in my room, so I rose up, thinking he would leave sooner. "Is your stomach still troubling you? He asked.

I repeated it in a shaky voice, despite the fact that he couldn't keep me out of school the next day. That sort of stuff was my mother's responsibility, not his.

"It could be hemorrhoids," he explained. "Have you ever thought about that?"

Looking back as an adult, I wonder what kind of youngster gets hemorrhoids? What would they do with his stomach? At the moment, however, I had no idea what he was talking about.

"Come into the bathroom," he said. "The one upstairs, not the one down here."

I returned my guinea pig to her pen and followed my father upstairs. He closed the bathroom door and locked it. Then he commanded me to pull my shorts and underwear down and lean over the sink counter. My father spent a lot of time in his underwear. He was actually in them right now. Most evenings, they wore briefs rather than boxers, paired with a white or blue button-down work shirt. His tie was loose and hung around his neck like a noose.

Aside from him rushing around the house in only half his clothes, we were a quite modest group. Dad seeing my buttocks made me uneasy, but I followed his instructions. I believe he chose the upstairs bathroom due to its layout. It was constructed such that I could bend forward with my head in the sink as he sat on the toilet, lid down, with a clear, well-lit view of, well, my asshole. "Spread your legs," he instructed. "Wider." He did not add anything. He just stared at it, as if it were a gem or something.

"All right," he replied after a while. "You can pull your pants back up."

This happened at least two more times in my youth, according to my memory: stomachache, bathroom visit, and anal examination.

When I told it to Hugh years later, he said, "Did you tell anyone?"

"Of course not," I replied. "I mean, it was embarrassing."

When I was fourteen, I awakened one morning to discover blood in my panties. It terrified me out. Where did it originate from, and why? I wondered.

Normally, I would have told Mom about it. Worried that she might tell my father and force me to bend over the sink again, I buried my underpants under some leaves in the steep ravine outside our house. Over the years, many different things have been buried there, and not just mine.

My father was weird in a variety of ways. When my oldest sister, Lisa, received her first bra, he summoned her to his seat at the head of the table. Then he stood up and slowly undid the buttons on her blouse, still wearing his underpants.

"Ha ha," everyone said. "Lisa is wearing a bra now! "

"Oh, Lou," my mother scolded.

When Gretchen and I were in high school, our parents brought us to New Orleans for the weekend. I believe it was my mother's idea, and we went on her expense, because we slept in a good hotel and had breakfast at Brennan's, which was a huge deal. The entire vacation was a big deal, and neither my sister nor I wasted a bit of it. Labelle's song "Lady Marmalade" had just been released and appeared to be playing everywhere. It was set in New Orleans, so we felt like we had an insider's perspective on the song, just like if we had been in Ventura, California, when the band America released "Ventura Highway" two years ago.

My father and I were on Bourbon Street, waiting for Gretchen and my mother, who had gone into a souvenir shop. "Lady Marmalade" was wafting out of a pub, and as they left and proceeded toward us, he commented of my sister, who was tottering on platform shoes, a straw hat on her head, and looking a lot like Jodie Foster in Taxi Driver, "God, she's got a great set of pins!" "

I had no idea what pins were, and when I found out they were legs, I thought, "That's a nice thing to say about someone." In general, I mean. If that person is not, say, your daughter. His voice had changed, wolfish, and the first word of his sentence—God—suggested remorse. Unfortunately, Gretchen was connected to him, thus he was unable to pursue her. It was a weird little moment, but I put it down to being out of town, to New Orleans, and "Voulez-vous coucher avec moi?" ", which our waiter at Galatoire's that evening interpreted as "Would you like to have some fun with me?" "

A few years later, he walked in on Gretchen and her boyfriend having sex in her basement bedroom, next to mine. When Jeff heard the door open, he rolled off the mattress and onto the floor, thinking he was out of sight. "Stand up," my father said.

Dad never looked at Gretchen in the same way again. Not long after, she went to the mall and had her photo taken at one of those studios that embossed its signature in the lower right-hand corner of the print, as if it were a piece of art. Olan Mills, I believe it was called. Everyone loved the photo except our father, who held it for a moment before tossing it aside, saying, "You look like a tired old whore."

There were countless other things our father did and said over the years. It was not that he violated our bodies. He simply wanted us to understand that they were as much his as ours. We simply ignored or laughed at his comments. "If only I were thirty-five years younger," he'd moan on the beach, seeing Amy in a bikini.

"That guy," we'd remark. "What a creeper! "

After we all left, he purchased several apartments near the university. The tenants were students, and he visited them on a regular basis, claiming to collect rent or perform minor repairs. "So I'm down on Clark Avenue to fix the hot water heater," he'd say, drink in hand at the end of the day, "and I walk into the upstairs bedroom to find Cal

Compton having sex with his girlfriend!" Can you believe it? "

"Did you knock first?" " we'd ask.

"What do I have to knock for? I own the place! "

He always acted so surprised. "So what do I find but Brenda Cash stepping out of her bathroom stark naked at, get this, three in the afternoon! " As if that were the story—that she didn't shower on his schedule.

We looked at all of this differently after our sister Tiffany accused our father of sexually abusing her. Our mother was long dead by this time. Tiffany was around forty and unemployed. When asked why she hadn't brought this up sooner, she said that it had been buried in her subconscious. It might have remained there, like a pharaoh's tomb, had her therapist not helped her unearth it.

"What exactly did Dad do? " we asked.

She said that she couldn't remember, but that didn't mean it didn't happen—in fact it was just the opposite. "It was obviously so awful that my mind shut down."

"OK," we answered, unsure. It wasn't like Lisa or Gretchen or Amy saying such a thing. Tiffany wasn't trustworthy the way they were. She wasn't sound.

As the years went, her story evolved slightly. Suddenly she remembered Dad entering her room in the middle of the night.

"He did that all the time," I reminded her. "Nothing drives him crazy than an open window with heat or air conditioning flowing out. You know how mental he goes over his power bill."

Amy shared a room with Tiffany, and she couldn't recall our father ever coming in after they were in bed. This is what occurs in a family when these types of charges are brought against someone. You think, Well, that couldn't have taken place here. Not in this house, the one where I had my asshole gazed at, the one where Lisa was allowed to pose topless. "Sure, Dad can be creepy," the rest of us responded, "but abuse? That's going too far! "

"If he's going to have sex with anyone, shouldn't it be Amy? "We asked one another. "No offense, but, I mean, she is prettier and a lot easier to handle."

Amy, Gretchen, and Lisa were always powerful, but to varying degrees. Tiffany was the vulnerable one.

In the aftermath of #MeToo, I understand how nasty this sounds, but it was difficult to accept much of what our sister said. By this point, we all felt Tiffany was insane. She lived just outside of Boston at the time, and her existence made little sense to us. Things that were important to me and the rest of my family—stability, affection, and having a lovely home—were not only irrelevant to her, but also demeaning. I know she used drugs—we all did at some point or another, some of us heavily—but the rest of us managed to keep our jobs. We did not search through each other's medication cabinets and swallow everything we found immediately away.

This is not meant to demean her. If anything, it strengthened her point. Isn't this what sexually abused individuals did? She was only missing specifics.

Tiffany had sex for money, as far as I know. "There's a guy who's paying me to fuck him with a strap-on dildo," she told me over the phone one afternoon, laughing. I was in Normandy, and she had called collect. "Now he wants to do it to me, so I'm wondering if you've ever used Anbesol to relieve the pain in your asshole. "

You never want your youngest sister to call for advice on anal sex, especially if she is being paid for it. I'm not sure why the last bit makes things worse, but it does.

"You are talking to the wrong person," I told her.

She considered for a moment. "Then put Hugh on the phone."

"He's the wrong person as well," I told him. "You need to call…another house."

Tiffany's early life appeared to have propelled her beyond the dating and puppy-love phases that the rest of us experienced. There was one phase missing. Anyone could see it. This also made us wonder if anything had happened. Ask for specifics—"What exactly did Dad do?"—and she'd say, every time, "I never said he threw me against a 1957 Chevy and fucked me."

"Well, then…"

"That's not what I said, that he threw me against a Chevy and fucked me."

"Great. Now that that's cleared up, I'm just wondering…"

"He didn't fuck me against a Chevy."

"Then what exactly…? "

"I never said anything about him fucking me."

My dad did have a '57 Chevy, but Tiffany was only two years old when he got rid of it and bought a red '64 Mustang.

What our sister came to term "physical abuse," the rest of us merely thought of as punishment—not fun, definitely, but far from unique, at least in that age. It wasn't uncommon for my mother to slap one of us across the face. She didn't get mad, but maybe once a year the cobra would strike, and, hand on your red-hot cheek, you'd find yourself exclaiming, incredulously, as if you might be wrong about this, "Did you just slap me across the face?"

My father once clamped his hands around my neck, lifted me off the ground, and pinned me to the wall. My feet were off the floor, and until the laundry room was painted fifty-five years later, you could still see the smudges my shoes had made as I struggled in vain for purchase. He would smack me with paddles. He shoved me into trees and beat me over the head with heavy serving spoons, but I still wouldn't claim that he abused me, maybe because, if I ever have children myself—which is unlikely—I reserve the right to equally rough them up should the situation call for it. "Damned kids, going through my pockets and taking all my change," I'll thunder. "I reached in for a coin at the grocery store today and came out with nothing but a paper clip!"

In such situations, I always wished I could tell my father, "Keep your pants on for ten goddamn minutes and maybe we won't paw through them for money."

I'm not sure why some individuals can look back on such situations and laugh, while others cannot. Tiffany needed an explanation for why her life was so chaotic, one that didn't entail the despair and mental illness that have afflicted both sides of our family for decades and will unjustly infect one person but not the next. As the years passed and parenting became a word, behavior that was once acceptable enough—calling your child a loser, flogging them with a belt or a switch—was perceived in a different light. We who were beaten and belittled frequently reflect upon it with something similar to pride. It testifies to our resilience and our ability to forgive. Not Tiffany, however. To her, it was a crime.

"So, I saw this mom smack her daughter on the street the other day, and do you think I contacted the cops?" She asked me over the phone one night. "Fuck no! Instead, I approached her and asked, 'Hey, why don't you let me watch your fucking kid for a while?' And you know,

David, if everyone did that, we wouldn't have had to grow up the way we did."

Tiffany might be really grandiose, like, "Stand back while I save the world." That being said, who is going to hand up her daughter to a complete stranger who simply used the word fucking before kid?

Tiffany began telling others after we stopped talking in 2004 that I had abused her and that she had always been terrified of me.

"Really?" I responded when Lisa informed me.

I recall inserting pins in Tiffany's ass while she was seated in the butterfly chair—the best spot in front of the basement TV—and I wanted to get her out of it. But it wasn't something I did every day, and I was only about ten years old. I recall riding her around her buckteeth, calling her a beaver, and so on, but we were children.

Tiffany was twelve when I left for college, and a few years later, she ran away from home. The police apprehended her, and she fled again a week later. This put her in Élan, a behavior modification center in Maine that claimed to be a school, despite the fact that the students/inmates only had one hour of class each day. They spent the remainder of their time bringing irreparable harm to one another. It's astounding how many graduates, including my sister, have committed suicide.

After two years of suffering, she returned to Raleigh and enrolled in a different high school, one where she didn't know anyone. Her grades were mostly Fs, and I am not sure if she graduated. I remember her spending nights at my apartment, usually after a fight with our parents. Like me, she had never learned to drive, so someone would bring her over.

Tiffany was a lively individual. Her voice was husky. She laughed readily and could communicate with everybody. This made her a hit at the upscale grocery store where she began working after school. She had only been there for six months when a customer approached her about working for Neuhaus Chocolates. Tiffany moved to New York and stayed for three years. She remained in Harlem. She stayed in Midtown with a Jewish female she described as insane. She lived with a coke dealer in Queens. One evening at a nightclub, she was hurried to the hospital, where she discovered a baby the size of a troll doll living in one of her fallopian tubes. An operation was conducted. My parents flew up, and my father inquired, "So, was it a boy or a girl? "

"Oh, Lou," my mother scolded.

I appreciated that when the doctor went in and asked Tiffany if she had any questions regarding her recovery, she said, weakly, in front of Mom and Dad, "Yes. When can I have sex again? "

She might be quite humorous like that. During the chocolate years, I remember her visiting me in Chicago and getting high while giggling. We were high on pot, ecstasy, LSD, and cocaine, and I was hoping that things would improve for her and that she would be able to leave the dreadful reform school behind.

Toward the end of her life—the final few years—she would call our father and threaten to go public with her abuse story. "And the point is that she calls collect," Amy explained. "And he accepts the costs! "

When Dad questioned Tiffany for specifics, she'd answer, exactly like she'd told us, "I never said you fucked me against a 1957 Chevy. "That is not what I am saying."

She simply remembered him entering her room.

She once called our father and taped the discussion with the intention of suing him for wrecking her life. "Do you consider me sexy? " was one of the questions she posed him.

It was incredibly trashy. "I was going to give the money to charity," she said when questioned about it later. "I wasn't going to keep it for myself."

Another time, she flew home and hurled a hibachi at him. "Was it the one inside the carport? " our sister Gretchen inquired. "Did she break it?" I wanted the hibachi! "

By then, our father was barely supporting Tiffany, giving her enough to get by. At the time of her second, successful suicide attempt, she was living in a group home with two guys, both of whom had long fingernails and neither of whom smelled the odor of her decomposing body. She stayed in a sweltering, unair-conditioned room for five days. "Well, we're heavy smokers," they said when asked about it.

On the day Tiffany's body was discovered, I contacted my father and sobbed.

"Don't allow yourself get all emotional over it," he said. "She had a stinking awful life. Everyone dumped on her, but what's done is done."

During a phone call a few days later, he mentioned, "After your sister was defeated, I gave it some thought."

It was an unusual word to use: conquered. Defeated.

Among her documents we discovered a letter she had written to our father. In it, she apologized for killing herself and expressed gratitude for everything he had done for her.

There can't be anything worse than losing a kid, yet shouldn't our father have felt relieved? This individual who called you every morning and harangued and threatened you is no longer with you. The automobile alarm that belonged to your daughter has finally been turned off, and the cable has been severed.

We continue to ponder about her accusations even after she died. Our father may be improper, especially by today's standards, but it did not necessarily make him a pedophile. However, his behavior did not help his case. To the rest of us, that was, if not typical, at least him—the way he'd take us to McDonald's, for example, and say to the counter girl if she was overweight, "Well, hey there, Porky."

"Dad," we would say, mortified.

He would just laugh. "She's out of shape, and someone needs to tell her as much."

If he thought a woman was attractive, he would say so. And if one was awful, he'd cringe, just like you would if you were seeing an accident. That was the worst, in his opinion. "There's nothing...feminine there," he'd complain, recalling a bank teller or supermarket cashier who didn't meet his expectations. "Nothing of beauty."

He was always watching my sisters' weight and attractiveness. When Lisa was sixty-three, she informed our father that she had shed twenty pounds. "Do you know what he said? " she asked. "'Lose any more and you and me are going to have a love affair.'"

"That's an excellent incentive! "I said. "Slim down to one-fifty, and you finally get to have sex with a 95-year-old man who is also your father! "

"I have the most beautiful girls on the block," he would boast in the 1970s and early 1980s. "By far." "No one else comes close."

At the country club, people would approach our table. "What good-looking daughters you have, Lou." I'd sit there in my red, white, and blue American flag tie, spectacles, and braces, thinking that with very little effort, they could have thrown my brother and me a bone, elevated that to "good-looking family." But it was true. My sisters were gorgeous. Part of me felt envious, but I was more proud. Families with ugly daughters do not count. That was something I learned very early on. We all did.

I imagine us at the country club on prime rib night. The girls—Dad's prizes—dressed up, and he kept an eye on them as they glided to and from the buffet, making sure they didn't overdo it with the ambrasia salad. I think about Tiffany. I recently visited a hotel dining room. I'd finished my dinner and approached a group of strangers: a mother, a father, and four children aged twelve to eighteen, all well-dressed and groomed, none of them on their phones, and all of them energetic and interested. "What a beautiful family you have," I told the parents. Then, fearing that I had crossed a boundary, I hurried awkwardly out the door and back to my room.

CHAPTER 10
SUMMER TEETH

𝒜 month into New York City's stay-at-home rule, I went for an afternoon walk and ended up following a man along Madison Avenue. The guy was a few inches taller than me, unimpressive in terms of dress, and I would not have noticed him if he hadn't cleared his throat and spat on the sidewalk. I was only staring at it—the nerve of some folks! —when a young woman turned the corner and came our way. She, like me, was wearing a mask, so I was astonished when the man said, "Hey, lovely. Why don't you smile? "

Did you actually just say that? I wanted to ask. For starters, he had no idea she was smiling, and secondly, hadn't the #MeToo movement taught even the most arrogant among us that women despise being told what to do with their faces?

I could not stand wearing a mask. It gave the city a smell similar to my breath, which had hints of milk and house paint. I was troubled by the uniformity it produced. Central Park, the Lower East Side, the Greek district in Queens where I purchase cheese, and Coney Island all smelled the same now.

My mask at the time was blue gingham. It was presented to me by my sister Amy and was designed to suit a petite woman rather than a slightly smaller male. The cloth was comfortable, but the straps were extremely tight, making my ears jut out like Pringles on hinges.

Still, I reminded myself that I wasn't the only one suffering. Whenever I couldn't take it any longer, I'd think of all the people who may have embraced a mask—like this woman I once read about in a book. She was on a tour of Antarctica, and when she stooped down to examine a baby leopard seal, it sprang up and bit her nose. The entire thing. So, for her, a face mask would have been really helpful. For the first time in years, she'd appear just like everyone else she passed on the street. It was the same for persons with cleft palates or really weak chins.

I'm quite self-conscious about my teeth, so the mask was a nice respite from the scrutiny I experienced in the United States. I'm not convinced you fit here; I could see the clerks were thinking in nice shops and hotels. If you actually had money, wouldn't you spend some of it at a dentist's office? It might have been worse, I guess. My teeth were mainly there and accounted for. Still, I'd be delusional to believe they weren't the first thing people noticed about me.

It was not always this way. I had braces when I was younger, and when they were removed around the age of seventeen, I looked great. Then I ruined everything by not wearing my retainer properly. By the age of twenty, I noticed a little gap between my front teeth, which increased over time. I could put a credit card in there first, followed by a library card. Then the edge of my wallet. Next, I developed gaps between the teeth next to the front ones. My top jaw has just so much space, thus the incisors began to protrude. "You look like you swallowed a bomb and your face froze a fraction of a second after it went off," Amy stated to my satisfaction.

What do people who don't have sisters do? Contact someone like my friend Scott. "You have summer teeth," he told me once.

I asked, "Excuse me? "

"Summer here; summer there," he explained.

A person other than me might have noticed this on his own, but I can't stare at my open lips. It's the only officially recognized phobia I have. When the pandemic began, I had not seen my teeth in nearly forty years. In photos, I'd smile broadly but keep my lips together, like a Peanuts character, and I'd never watch a video of myself.

When conversing, I usually hide my mouth, especially if the other person has lovely teeth, which are always the first thing I notice about them. Even pets. "Poor thing," a buddy once said about his cat. "Cromwell just went to the vet and had all of his premolars and canines removed."

Ha ha, I thought, feeling very superior. To the cat.

America is a difficult place to be if you're self-conscious about your grin, especially in some sections of the country, such as Southern California. I used to believe that people wore dark glasses because it was difficult to drive with the light in their eyes. More than likely, the shine of an incoming driver's teeth blinds them. This is why I feel so at ease in Japan, where dental standards appear to be non-existent and people have worn masks for years. The most terrifying lips I've ever seen was on a clerk in a Tokyo department store. The woman's top central incisors expanded forward from her gums like tusks, forming a dark, uneven shelf on which her upper lip rested.

I told an oral surgeon in London, "You'd think a Japanese dentist could have helped her out for free, just as a project."

"Someone most likely offered to," he replied. "But when someone is that far gone, it's usually due to a phobia. They refuse to go in for treatment, even if it is free."

The surgeon's notion was tested a few weeks later in West Sussex. I was at a thrift store in a village close to my house. The clerk was young and cheery, and when he opened his mouth to greet me, I noticed the second-worst teeth I'd ever seen. Some were broken off, while others were gone. There were gray ones and black ones, one straight and the next at an odd angle, like a mouthful of pebbles—which surprised me because he was otherwise so attractive. It was a lot to process, and I assumed he could feel my gaze focusing on that region of his face, just as someone with an awful birthmark could.

I can be very impulsive, which is risky when combined with an excessive discretionary cash. "Oh, what the hell," I said not long ago, agreeing to a $3,000 thick black sport coat with layers of ruffles pouring over the hem. Should I explain that it didn't fit me and never will unless I have all of my ribs removed?

My impulsive behavior spreads to others as well. During a book signing, I began asking people if they spoke a foreign language. This was in Reno, Nevada, a city whose attractions are not immediately apparent to the casual observer. "I speak a little Spanish," someone may claim, or "I had a semester of German in college."

I eventually met a young woman who had completed six years of French. She had gone to my event alone and was exactly the type of reader I had envisioned when I first began writing.

"Have you gone to Paris? "I asked.

She declined, and when I asked why, she gave me the exact look I would have given myself forty years ago. "I am a barista with student debt. "I can't afford a plane ticket halfway around the world."

"Then I'm going to buy you one," I told you.

When Hugh was this young woman's age, he went to Paris alone and concluded he'd rather die than return home. He began attending French classes and eventually secured employment as a cook for an elderly couple. That led to friendships, new professions, and a full life. I pictured the same thing happening to this young woman. She only needed someone to open the door.

This, I've always believed, is the entire point of having money: to transform people's lives.

"But who were you to say her life needed to change? " Hugh inquired after I informed him about her. "You knew her for all of five minutes."

The young woman waited six months to earn what she thought was a reasonable amount of spending money. Then she boarded the plane and flew to Paris. A few days into her stay, she visited a café with a view of Notre Dame and sent me an email. In it, she stated that she had arrived safely and would give anything to be back in Reno, sitting on her front porch and sipping Jack Daniel's with a pickle juice chaser. The vacation I had funded had taught her a valuable lesson: there is no place like home.

This was not the first time I had tried anything like this. It wouldn't be the last. Of course, when someone begs for my assistance, I rarely offer it, believing that it must be my idea. I had been thinking about the young man at the charity shop for a few weeks before returning one afternoon and pulling him aside. "Listen," I continued, "I don't want to humiliate you, and I understand how unusual this may sound, but I'd like to pay to get your teeth corrected. I don't expect anything in return—you and I don't need to communicate again. We can arrange this with a local dentist. He or she will send me the bills, and I will deal with them."

The young man blinked.

"Are you twenty-three years old?" I guessed. "

"Twenty-four," he said.

"The point is that you have your whole life ahead of you," I said later. "This could change everything."

I'd only learn later how suspicious I sounded. Before going to the charity shop, I had been picking up litter along the roadside. And so I dressed as if I lived outside. My shirt, which was untucked and tattered, was stained with mud and dried blood from digging deep into blackberry bushes for empty bottles and cans that people leave there. My arms and neck were scratched. I looked and smelled like I'd just fought a cheetah over an antelope carcass. Then there were the contents of my own mouth, the teeth arranged like tombstones in a church cemetery. If you want to pay for someone else's dental work, you should definitely start with your own, as the young man, whom I'll name Denton, was undoubtedly thinking.

"Well," he answered, "a lady I talked to once mentioned something about dentures—"

"You don't want dentures," I informed him. "They are a pain in the ass. Implants, on the other hand, are truly amazing in terms of their capabilities. Please let me take care of this for you." I jotted down my name and email address. "I know how crazy this sounds, believe me."

He accepted the slip of paper I offered. "I don't know what to say."

I shrugged. "Say yes."

"And you honestly expected him to take you up on it? " My friend Adam inquired a few months later, when I told him about it.

"Sure," I replied. "I mean, an offer like that is only going to come once in a lifetime."

He laughed. "That might be true, but you sounded like an old pervert."

Hugh held the same opinion.

"But I specifically told him I didn't want anything in return," I explained, realizing as the words left my mouth that that's exactly what an old pervert would say, especially one with scratch marks on his neck and dried blood on his shirt. "Still, he could have googled me," I reasoned. "I've never looked myself up, but surely there must be something about me online that's positive, or at least not so horribly negative that someone wouldn't trust me to pay for his implants."

I haven't been back to the charity shop since the afternoon I volunteered my assistance, and I doubt I will return in the future. I've passed Denton on the street twice, and while we exchanged greetings, it seemed strange. I don't want to make things worse by pressing him, though I often think of what a difference this could have made in his life. Then again, who am I to decide that his life needs improving? He struck me as a genuinely lovely person, so perhaps his friends and family—the ones who truly matter—see only that: his decency.

The epidemic struck just when I was about to give up hope of hearing from Denton. If wearing a mask altered how the world perceived me—someone who, given my age, is essentially invisible—I can only image what it did for him. Talking to people and not noticing their gaze fixed on your mouth, having them look you in the eye and think, Hey, who is he? That had to feel nice for him. I know it happened to me. So much so that when dentist offices reopened, I went to one in New York, a Greek woman suggested by a friend, and received braces—at the age of 64. They weren't the metal ones I'd worn as a youngster, but rather a new sort made of transparent plastic. They're called Invisalign, and I first heard about them from my niece. She had purchased them herself and indicated that she replaced them every two weeks and discarded the old ones.

Can you give these to me to wear? "I asked. In terms of idiotic questions, this ranks right up there with "Do you think mankind might one day live peacefully on the sun?". "

The first step in receiving my personal Invisalign aligners was having my mouth scanned. This was done by a technician who used a wand that appeared to be meant for a considerably larger mouth, possibly that of a lion. The result was a 3D representation of my teeth and gums that the dentist could edit, allowing me to see how I would appear after only fourteen weeks of therapy. My spring lecture tours had been canceled, so I didn't have to be anyplace or do a lot of talking. And I would have to wear them solely on top. So, why not?

The Invisaligns arrived in early April, in seven installments, each in its own plastic envelope with a date on it. Every other Thursday, I was supposed to put on a new one and wear it for at least 22 hours a day, only taking it off for meals. The first time you insert a new one, your teeth say, loudly, "WHAT THE FUCK DO YOU THINK YOU'RE DOING? " However, they stop talking after a few hours. I was scared about talking funny, but the change was minor. At worst, I sounded slightly intoxicated.

I was born without a left lateral incisor, and my teenage braces forced everything together, removing the vacant area. The aim was to recreate the vacant spot and replace it with a false tooth. Even with my Play-Doh gums, it was surprising how quickly my teeth seemed to move. I could feel the difference on my tongue but couldn't force myself to look.

"What exactly are you terrified of? Hugh inquired. "Honestly, so what if your teeth are black? "

I went into a panic. "Are they? "

"Why don't you see for yourself?" "

But I couldn't, even when my dentist advised me to during a mid-Invisalign checkup.

"What's up with these molars?" " she inquired, pushing around in the back of my lips. "They seem to be awfully flat."

"Like cows'? "

She considered for a moment. "Or a donkey's."

Ah, Greeks.

The fourteen weeks went by fast and without incident. Braces cost more time than money. They're clear, so I spent many hours searching for where I'd left them. They blended in seamlessly, like chameleons, on the blanket, the desk, and over Hugh's soiled T-shirt with Snoopy on it. On the scheduled date, I returned to the dentist, who appeared pleased with the way things had changed. That afternoon, my gap would be filled with an artificial tooth, and crowns would be fitted to its three closest neighbors. To attach them, three incisors had to be filed to thin, pointed posts that looked like the teeth of a juvenile alligator. "I never let people look at themselves in this condition," the dentist remarked. "If they tell me they have to go to the bathroom, I say, 'Sorry, but you'll have to hold it.' Because shaved-down teeth—what you have in your mouth right now—are impossible to unsee once you've seen them."

I sat in the chair for over three hours, and when the dentist brought me the mirror at the end of the session, I held it in front of me, gathered my courage, and opened my mouth. All I wanted was for the sight to remain unremarkable. Not perfect or blinding, but typical for a man my age.

"What did his teeth look like?" "Someone could ask.

And you would respond, "Gosh, I didn't notice. "He has terrible bags under his eyes, though."

What I saw before me was better than unremarkable, though my opinion may alter over time. As it was, the view was clouded with pride, the kind you get when you refinish a piece of furniture or rebuild a kitchen, though in this case I'd done none of the work myself, merely ordered it to be done and tolerated the minor inconvenience while it was being done.

"Now, let me show you your 'before' pictures," the dentist explained. She took out her phone, and I saw what appeared to be the jaws of a hippo in attack mode. Summer teeth, indeed. How had I chewed the food?

"And I was wandering around like this? "I asked.

She placed the phone away. "Apparently."

My new teeth must have looked great when, a few minutes later, the receptionist handed me a $14,000 bill for one day's work, and my mouth dropped agape.

Back in the flat, I grinned so warmly at Hugh that my eyes vanished.

Hugh looked at me and said, "I liked you better before."

Amy said the same thing. "Your old teeth had character."

"Yes, but you didn't have to live with them," I informed her. "The guy who pushes himself along on a dolly has character too, but that doesn't mean he shouldn't get a set of functioning legs if he wants them."

Amy had visited our apartment for a celebration dinner. Hugh made spaghetti, and for the first time in forty years, I was able to put a forkful in my mouth and cleanly bite it off, exactly like any other person. Previously, the strands would get trapped in my gaps, forcing me to nibble on them like a dog.

It took me a while to quit concealing my mouth when speaking. Hold on, I'd think, glancing at the teeth of whoever I was speaking with. If anyone should be humiliated, it's him.

I also realized how having ordinary teeth increased my confidence. Now, when my credit card didn't go through, I'd respond calmly, "Maybe if you try it again." In the past, I'd start sweating, not because I'd done anything wrong, but because my gaps made me appear to have. I felt more at ease checking into a good hotel. I felt as if the slate had been wiped clean, and the world could now judge me based on the awful things I said rather than how shitty I looked while saying them.

When a woman told me during a book signing that I had a great smile, I truly considered crying. I never expected to hear it from someone. It would have been like receiving a compliment on my hair, which would only happen if the rest of the world grew bald and I now possessed something they lacked.

How foolish of me not to have done this sooner. I had expected it to take years, and that I'd be one of those unhappy adults with a mouthful of metal, yet it only took three and a half months from start to finish.

I think about that young man in England, who has his entire life ahead of him. I think about how much my most recent dental work cost. Next, I double it, figuring how much I would have paid if both my top and bottom teeth needed to be worked on. Then I pray that he misplaced the slip of paper on which I typed my name and email address.

CHAPTER 11
THE SPLINTERS BENEATH MY SKIN

*T*en days before his death, my father had a little stroke and fell. Or possibly he fell and subsequently had a stroke. In any case, I was shocked when others enquired about the cause of death. He was ninety-eight! Wasn't that enough?

I went to see him shortly after his fall, flying down from New York with Amy and Hugh. Gretchen and Paul met us at Springmoor, but he was mostly gone by then. There was a livid gash on his forehead, and he was propped up in his bed, which appeared terribly short, like a cut-down one from a department store. His eyes were wide, his mouth open, and a shimmering curtain of spittle trailed behind his lips.

"Dad? "Amy said.

An assistant approached and shook his leg. "Mr. Sedaris? Lou? You have some family here to visit you." She stared at us before returning her gaze to our father. "He's pretty much been this way for a while now." Another leg shaking. "Mr. Sedaris? "

In reaction, our father gulped for air.

"Well, he looks good," Amy answered, drawing a chair to his bedside.

Who does she compare him to? I wondered. Google "old man dying," and I'm sure you'll see what we saw: an unconscious skeleton with only a little meat on it, moaning.

You always believe that if you gather around and concentrate, the person on the bed will let go. You see yourself telling your buddies, "We were all there." And it was strangely beautiful. So you turn solemn and sit quietly, watching the chest unsteadily rise and fall. You see the hands as they sporadically stir, performing some fictitious last-minute busywork. The oxygen tube slips, and you consider readjusting it, but you don't because it has snot on it. It's better to preserve it for an aide, you convince yourself. After around twenty minutes, your sister Gretchen steps outside. Hugh exits the room, followed by Paul. You go out and find them all in the open-air courtyard, seated in rocking chairs, Gretchen starting a cigarette. "Did I tell you that we are no longer allowed to say native plants at work?" "She asks.

She's the only one in the family who works as a horticulture for the city of Raleigh, which means she has a boss to report to and countless, needless meetings that take up her important time. Gretchen talks about work a lot, but I always enjoy hearing it. "What did you say when you were told that? " I ask.

"Nothing," she says. "I simply went out. I mean, this is insane! "

Amy arrives about a minute later.

"Now people are calling for gender-neutral toilets in the city parks," Gretchen says. "There isn't enough money in the budget to create them, so the few bathrooms that do exist will probably be designated as unisex. "I suppose this solves the problem, but I prefer having a separate women's room." She crushes her cigarette. "Men's bathrooms always smell like shit."

"And the women's smell like vomit," Amy says.

"Do they really?" " I inquire, concerned that my father may die while we are all sitting outdoors discussing how bad public restrooms smell.

"God, yes," Gretchen says. She digs into her purse and takes out a palm-sized black book. "Here." She hands it to me. "I found this at Dad's house a few days ago and saved it for you."

I mistake it for a pocket Bible, super-abridged, with only the good bits included, and then I think, "What good parts?" I realize it's for addresses, and it's my father's Little Black Book, as the color and size suggest. "It must have been from before he went to Syracuse and started writing in all capital letters," she explains.

I open it to see about fifty names, followed by addresses and phone numbers, mostly of women, with a remark next to them.

Returning to the room, I glance at my father, who appears to be asleep, and wonder if he had sex with these women or merely tried. Why weren't any of them Greek, and what does advanced mean? I bring it up with Hugh a few hours later, after we leave Springmoor and head to the beach. "If Patty O'Day and Dorothy Castle are still alive, do you think they remember him? "

"I guess it depends on what went on," Hugh says. "Anyway, I'm sure you can ask your father about it the next time you see him."

We pass a low brick house with a tattered TRUMP flag in the front yard. "The next time I see him, he'll be dead," I reply.

Hugh frowns. "You don't realize that. "I mean, he's come through before."

This occurred on a Sunday in late May. Six days later, Springmoor contacted and informed me that my father had stopped eating and was on morphine. By then, my sister Lisa and her husband, Bob, as well as my friend Ronnie and Hugh's friend Carol, had joined us in the Sea Section. That night, we went to supper in Atlantic Beach. "Dad is going to die while we're eating," I remarked as we left the house. The evening was hot and humid, more like summer than spring.

"David! " Hugh scolded.

"I'm not wishing," I informed him, "just predicting."

And properly, it turned out. Lisa received the call just as we were completing our appetizers. There was no music playing at the Island

Grille, but because the space was small and full to capacity, it was too loud to hear the Springmoor representative on the other end. Lisa stepped outside, and I followed a few minutes later. "Dad's dead," she murmured as I closed the screen door behind me.

She was sitting on a bench, and as I took my place next to her, a young couple exited the restaurant hand in hand and made their way to their car, stopping to kiss beneath a streetlamp along the way. The male was lean, bearded, and significantly taller than the young woman. As she reached on her toes to reach his mouth, her skirt rose to reveal her panties. "Look at what that girl is wearing," Lisa exclaimed, holding the phone in her lap with half of Paul's number put into it.

"It's certainly short," I remarked, following her gaze. "But it works for her."

Lisa breathed out and finished dialing. "If you say so."

She notified Paul that our father had died, and I informed the others. Receiving such a call is something you ponder about your entire life. When does it happen, and where will I be? You wonder. There is a responsibility in delivering such news, but the more times you call and get someone's voice mail, the less solemn you will be. In the end, I sounded more pissed off than anything. "Where have you been?" "Dad has died."

Gretchen was very difficult to call, and I didn't reach her until the next morning. We spoke for a bit, then she called me back a few hours later, seeming practically stoned. "I'm just wandering around in a daze," she told me.

"I hear that's fairly normal," I assured her, peering out the sliding glass door at the peaceful, green water.

"I mean...I could be coming into some serious money!" "She continued.

So, for her, I was the bringer of good news.

When our mother died, my siblings and I plunged headfirst into a dark pit. The first several days were the darkest. It remained the same after our sister Tiffany committed suicide. However, with our father, things were different. By the time the check arrived at the Island Grille that night, we had moved on to other topics: gas stoves versus electric stoves, a funny vampire-themed TV show, and Lisa eating an entire gallon of ice cream with her bare hands while driving home from the grocery store, clawing it out of the carton with her increasingly numb fingers. Perhaps we went so readily to other things because, given my father's advanced age, this moment was expected. Then he was Lou Sedaris. By the second half of his ninety-seventh year, the guy was a pussycat, a joy. Unfortunately, there were all those years before it. His death did not cause the world to slow down, much alone stop—not even for his family.

A month before our father's stroke, Amy and I searched through a box of photos and found what we believed would be the ideal obituary photo: Dad at his fiftieth birthday party, standing in his basement with a ghutra on his head. It could have been a white dishcloth, but the band holding it in place was convincing, as were his tanned skin and joined hands. He appeared to be a Saudi official taking a brief break from brokering a peace accord or ordering the assassination of a journalist. Our second runner-up featured him with long, thin Willie Nelson braids. They were artificial, affixed to a headband, and placed on him by Paul. The photos made him appear much more entertaining than he was. They did him a favor.

"Ummm, no," Lisa answered when it came time to contact the newspaper. "I want something that people will recognize." The one she chose was an old person's senior class photo, a snapshot of our father at age ninety-six, withered and lost-looking, photographed at Springmoor.

This is how animosity grows after someone dies: one decision at a time. The obituary was similarly bland—basically a résumé. I didn't really want to write it. Neither did Paul, Gretchen, or Amy. None of us could have done the innumerable things Lisa did, such as contacting the funeral home, cleaning out our father's room at Springmoor, and phoning his bank and lawyer. He requested a funeral in the Greek Orthodox Church. This meant that he couldn't be cremated, therefore a casket had to be purchased and clothing selected.

Most people I know would prefer to be disposed of with as little ceremony as possible. My English friend Andrew, for example, has given his body to science. "I read an account somewhere or other of medical students using an old woman's intestines as a skipping rope," he told me not long after making his plans. "It shocked me at first, but I'll be dead when the time comes, so I probably won't mind it so much."

Andrew does not want a church service, but he would not mind if a few people came together for drinks or a lovely supper in his memory. In contrast, my father insisted on a three-state death tour. Gretchen and I both agreed: "It's a lot of running around for someone who couldn't be bothered to pick us up from the airport."

There was to be a funeral in Raleigh, a burial nearly a week later in my father's hometown of Cortland, New York, and a third service forty days later, a sort of "Don't think for one minute that you can forget me" type of thing, followed by a traditional dish of boiled wheat berries and pomegranate.

Greek Orthodox funerals, like Catholic funerals, are essentially masses. My father's funeral was held on a Tuesday morning at Holy Trinity, our childhood church. Paul resides in Raleigh, where Gretchen works. They could have simply driven to the service from their houses, but instead we all checked into a very expensive hotel in Cary and went all out, billing the estate for everything: room service, beverages, the works. The staff mistook us for wedding guests because we looked so happy as we walked to the church in our formal attire. "Could you snap our photo? " Amy questioned one of the doormen, handing him her phone. She appeared to be on her way to a Satanic ball. She donned a black, short dress with absurdly large sleeves. It had the texture of a thick paper towel and was certainly not sorrowful. In contrast, Paul appeared to work at an ice cream store.

"Dad's casket is cherry with brushed nickel trim," Lisa explained as we took our seats in the front pews. "And just to clarify, I had him clothed in his underwear, not a diaper. With regular pants on top, of course."

"Great," we responded, wondering how the casket she chose could possibly be any hideous. If it were a chair, it would have been high-backed and upholstered in burgundy corduroy. If it had been a lamp, it would have included a frosted hurricane shade. Just as the funeral began, two guys in suits opened the casket lid, showing our father from the sternum upwards. What struck me, as it did us all, was how small he was. His hands, which appeared to be barely larger than a ventriloquist's dummy, draped vampirically across his chest, while his face and hair were the eerie off-white of a button mushroom, complete with a tiny sheen. Amy described his appearance as "like he was carved out of makeup."

"That open-casket business is so tacky," I commented later, as we met for coffee and baklava in the church's multipurpose room. "If I had to go on exhibit after my death, I'd insist on being positioned facedown. Then there'd be only the back of my head to worry about."

Actually, I'd like to be cremated in a plain pine box painted by Hugh with an image or pattern of his choosing. I honestly believe that would be an ideal business for him. "People could live with their coffins for years, using them as blanket chests or bookshelves—even coffee tables," I said as we left the funeral. "A-Tisket, A-Casket, the company could be called."

After changing into our post-funeral attire, Amy, Gretchen, and I walked to the state park near our hotel. The afternoon was hot and bright. On our way over, we saw a furious stick figure of a man standing by a dog carrier and an overcrowded sack of clothing, shaking a scribbled placard at incoming automobiles. He wore no shirt and had tattoos on both arms and the backs of his hands. People had offered him food and water, but empty bags and plastic bottles covered the ground around him. As we approached, we could see the lean-to he'd built in a thicket, which was also overflowing with trash.

This prompted Gretchen to discuss the camps she and her team found on city property. "It's sad," she told me, "but if we don't clear them out, it's just one phone call after another, with people complaining about human shit and needles."

It was good to get to the park and escape the harsh heat, which was now obscured by a tall, bright canopy of leaves. It felt ten degrees cooler in the forest. The funeral seemed like a distant memory. We'd been strolling for about ten minutes when Gretchen abruptly stopped and knelt in front of a group of little plants with tattered white petals. "Look," she exclaimed, "pussytoes!" "

"They are what? "I asked.

"Antennaria plantaginifolia," she explained. "Pussytoes."

"Oh, that is going to be my password for everything from this moment on," Amy told our group. As she took out her phone to take a note, it rang, and she replied with a bright "Hi, Dad!" "

She said it so brightly and naturally that for a brief minute, I assumed it was all a trick, that the body we'd seen at the church was a double carved out of makeup, and our father was still alive. And I thought, "Fuck!"

Following my mother's death, if a witch had said, "I'll bring her back, but—," I would have answered, "Yes! " without waiting for the remainder of the sentence. And if Mom and I spent another twenty years together, with her being herself and me being, say, a deaf mouse forced to live in her underwear, I'd still consider it a fair trade.

My father, however, had a different narrative. One of the things I'd heard repeatedly at church that morning was, "Lou was a real character."

When a character reaches the age of eighty-five, he is considered to be an enormously difficult person. It's what Hitler and Idi Amin might have been dubbed if they had survived for another three decades. But there is a part you must play when a parent dies, so every time I heard it, I answered, "Yes, he was certainly unique."

"I know you're going to miss him terribly" was another frequently repeated line.

"Oh, goodness, yes," I'd reply—not a lie, precisely. I assume I'll miss him in the same way that I missed getting colds during the epidemic, but who knows how I'll feel a few years later?

People's parents used to die in their sixties and seventies, cleanly, of old-fashioned malignancies and heart attacks, leaving the child on his or her own around the age of forty-five. However, as individuals live longer lives, you can be a grandmother while still being someone's son or daughter. The woman across the road from us in Normandy was eighty years old when her mother died. That, to me, is terrifying. It is disfiguring to be a child for so long, especially if your relationship with that parent is strained. For years, I felt like one of those pollarded plane trees that I'll always connect with Paris, the kind that has been severely pruned since saplinghood and looks like a towering fist in the winter.

As long as my father had authority, he used it to harm me. In my youth, I simply took it. Then I started writing about it, hoping to benefit from it. The money was comforting, but the roar of live audiences as they laughed at his petty and arrogant behavior was even more so.

"Well, I feel sorry for him," Hugh has started to remark. "No one was born acting the way he did. Something must have happened to make him that cruel."

This is true, yet getting to the heart of my father was nearly impossible. He never responded to questions about his youth, simply responding, "What do you want to know that for? "

During one of the numerous prayer pauses at his funeral, I was on my knees but kept my eyes open, recalling the day I was invited to give the baccalaureate address at Princeton. These are difficult to write, at least for me. The audience is constantly fatigued, it's always terribly hot outside, and you're compelled to wear a black, thick robe with what appears to be a cushion on your head. I was about to deny the offer, but instead I called my father and told him that if he wanted to accompany me, I would. The Ivy League stuff piqued his interest—though, to be fair, it has always done so for me. People who attended Harvard, Princeton, or Yale are always incredibly discreet about it. "I went to school in the Boston area," they remark, or, "I think I spent some time in New Jersey once." If I had gone from a top-tier school, I would have found a way to incorporate it into every conversation I had.

"Would you prefer the coffee hot or iced? "

"Back at Columbia I always had it hot, but what the hell, let's try something new."

Now my father exclaimed, "Princeton!" Are you kidding? "I would love to go."

Prior to the graduation ceremony, we attended a luncheon and sat at a table with the university president. There were other people there, dignitaries of various stripes, and as our dinner arrived, my father—who had previously referred to Bill Clinton, who would be speaking the next day, as "Slick Willie"—told the president that she had made a terrible mistake. "You asked my son to give the speech, but you really want my daughter Amy. She would have the audience in the palm of her hands. They'd eat her up, I promise you. I have videotapes of her appearances on several talk shows that I can email you. Then you will see! Amy is the ticket, not David."

The university president cordially thanked him for the suggestion. Then she asked me a question about the lecture tour I had recently completed, and my father chimed in again. "I can see the graduates and their families now. They would go home and speak about her! They would tell all their pals! Amy is who you desire."

Is this why you came here with me? " I asked him later, as a car arrived to drive us to New York.

"Oh, don't pull that business," my father said. "The woman needed to know that she could have done better."

I was fifty years old at the time, and what stung was not my father's words—I was impervious by then—but the fact that he was still attempting to undermine me. I never faulted Amy for stuff like this. It was not her fault. Similarly, I never blamed Gretchen when I had an art show and he informed the organizers that the person they truly needed was his daughter Gretchen. "She's got the talent, not him."

He was constantly attempting to pit his children against one another, never realizing the kinship we shared. It was forged by having him as a father, and it remained valid as long as he lived. It is common to hear about families falling apart after a parent's death. Lifelong checks are no longer in place, therefore the equilibrium is thrown off. Slights become insurmountable. There are disagreements over the estate, etc. It's a difficult section of road.

Saul Bellow remarked, "Losing a parent is like driving through a plate-glass window. You didn't realize it was there until it cracked, and then you spent years picking up the pieces." I felt like I had gathered all of the big, easy-to-reach, apparent ones. The splinters, on the other hand, will undoubtedly take a long time—possibly my entire life. I could feel them beneath my skin as I paused with my sisters in this quiet, shaded valley, orphaned and alone amid the pussytoes.

CHAPTER 12
FIG ON THE CONCOURSE

*T*hroughout the worst of the pandemic, I, like everyone else, reflected on the many things I had taken for granted when life was normal: oh, to be handed an actual restaurant menu; to stand so close to a stranger that you can read the banal text messages that are obviously more important to him than his toddler stumbling off the curb and into traffic.

Many people felt they had taken their employment for granted, but I did not. I've always enjoyed my profession, or at least the parts of it that were public and required reading aloud. The last show I did before COVID took my job was in Vancouver, British Columbia, at a rock house with a grim, cramped lobby and the kind of dressing room you see in movies about performers who overdose on drugs because their dressing rooms are so depressing. However, the crowd was great, and I enjoyed my stay, which is really what it is all about. I'm never the one who pays for the room, so I'm spared the part where you lie awake, wondering if it's really worth six, seven, or eight hundred dollars only for someone to sneak in while you're away and arrange a pair of slippers next your newly turned-down bed. They're on the carpet and appear to belong to a wealthy ghost who has just moved aside to make place for you.

The next morning, in the restaurant of my Vancouver hotel, I sat next to a lovely actor who I recognized immediately. He was quick-tempered and physically aggressive in the most recent television series I had seen him in, so I appreciated how courteous he was to the server and the woman who floated away with his empty orange-juice glass. "Oh, thank you. That's incredibly nice of you.

As I boarded the elevator back to my room, the hotel manager approached me and inquired how my stay was going. "Terrific," I said. "I just saw a big star in the restaurant."

"I can't confirm that," the man answered, with a forced smile.

"I don't need you to," I replied, smiling back. "I know perfectly well who it was."

Then I couldn't remember the guy's name for the life of me. "Oh, you know," I remarked to my friend Adam, who had produced the previous evening's event and drove me to the airport about an hour after I finished my breakfast. "It was what's his name who's on that TV series with the woman who used to be married to the guy who made that movie with a song in it that everybody knows."

Aside from the star sighting, my last event was rather standard. I read something new and discovered that it did not operate as well as I had hoped. Then I spent three hours signing books. The evening was unremarkable—which is a shame because for the next year and a half, I would obsess about it, practically fetishizing it. That was what I used to do for a living, I believe. And now it is over. On the best days, I'd remind myself that everyone was at home, and that this was only a temporary setback. A part of me was concerned, however, that when the world inevitably went on, it would do so without me, or at least with no special need for me. The circus would travel again, but not with this elephant.

From the onset of the pandemic, I determined not to get Zoom. "What exactly do you mean by 'get' it? Hugh inquired. "There is nothing you need to buy or attach to your computer. "You press a button, and it's there."

"Can you mark which button? "I asked. "I want to make sure I never push it."

Over the next eighteen months, I did one Zoom event, but it was not on my computer. Someone came to the flat, and I used his instead.

"How did it go?" "My lecturing agent inquired when it was over.

"I have no idea," I told him. And it was true. Without a live audience—that unknowing gathering of fail-safe editors—I'm lost. I am interested in the quality of their stillness as well as their laughing. In terms of noises, I believe a groan is always appropriate. A cough indicates that if they were reading this part on the page, they would be skimming right now, whereas a snore represents your brother-in-law holding a gun to your head and firing the trigger.

Of course, I wrote throughout the pandemic. I published things, which was scary because I had no idea whether they worked or not until a public reading. I can occasionally attempt anything on Hugh, but only for a short while. He'll listen for about a minute before turning away and claiming he'd prefer read it himself, and only after the book or magazine is published.

"Yes, but by then it'll be too late to make changes," I informed him.

Hugh and I have completely different senses of humor—that is, I have one while he does not. What I need him for are the You can't say thats and You're disgustings he'll interrupt me with on the rare instances when I make it past the first paragraph.

Hugh's statement, "That's terrible," is a clear guarantee that the crowd will laugh. Congressman Prude, one of my many nicknames for him, is well-deserved. "I just don't see the need for that language," he'll sniff, referring to the term "bare bottom" one time and ovaries the next. "Do you have to speak that way?"

During my tour, I was frequently told that I was overworked, despite the fact that all I had done that day was eat breakfast and fly from Atlanta to Birmingham for an hour. That is not at all exhausting. There were definitely some tough days. Flights would be canceled, and alternate routes would be quickly planned. But I wasn't doing the configuring. Rather, it was a travel agent, a professional. I'd see hotheads in those interminable customer-service lines where each passenger needed a whole half hour of phone calls and intense keyboard tapping, but that was never me. I outsourced the drama to someone else, so even if it resulted in a chaotic rerouting, I couldn't complain.

During the worst of the pandemic, I flew about a dozen times, including trips to North Carolina, Indiana, Kentucky, and the United Kingdom. It grieved me to see the airports so empty, with the majority of companies shuttered and lounges closed. While strolling through Charlotte Douglas International one afternoon in the summer of 2020, I noticed what appeared to be a fig laying on the floor on one of the nearly vacant concourses. When I looked closer, I saw it was a turd—probably a dog's. What has the world come to? I thought. It was like seeing my office in disarray. The airport was my destination. I knew its rhythms and norms, and I could tell the difference between professional and rookie travelers as soon as they got out of their automobiles, the latter with their squishy neck pillows holding up TSA checks. "I knew I couldn't go through with water, but what about Sprite? "

I would be at precheck, not bothered by the newbies but enraged nonetheless. I suppose you don't realize how nice it feels to look down on someone until you're both indiscriminately kicked to the curb.

I couldn't wait to go back on my high horse, and I eventually had the opportunity in the fall of 2021. My lecture agent had organized a seventy-two-city tour that would begin the second week of September. I got my old life back, sort of. There would be restrictions: in jurisdictions that permitted such activities, the audience would be required to produce proof of vaccination, and everyone would be masked. I tried not to get my expectations up too much, but I also needed to be prepared in case things went my way. If the elephant was going back out with the circus, he needed to be a little less elephant-like. I'd gained about twenty pounds over the previous year and a half and would need to shed them if I wanted to fit into my tour clothing. I devised a regimen that included walking fifteen miles each day, eating half as much as usual, and indulging in as much sugar-free Jell-O as I desired.

People asked, "Which flavor? "

However, there are no flavors, only colors: red, green, yellow, orange, and a new beige one that tastes beige. It was insane how quickly I lost weight. Every other week, I would take my belt to the cobbler and have another hole punched. At first, he said, "Congratulations!" Then it was, "You again? "

I was just relieved that he recognized me, as I felt much older now.

"I think it's your clothes that are the giveaway," the man replied. And it is true. Consider Harry Truman dressed similarly to Dolley Madison during the White House years.

Two days before my tour began, the first city was canceled owing to concerns regarding the Delta version. I was worried that the others would fall like dominoes, but Nashville held strong. It was exciting to be in front of an audience again, to expend energy and have it reverberate back. To stay in a nice hotel! Over the next three months, I discovered that several of them had reduced their services—a daily room cleaning had to be specially requested, purportedly for COVID reasons but actually due to a lack of housekeepers. In city after city, I saw only HELP WANTED signs. If McDonald's offered $14 per hour, Taco Bell next door was willing to pay $16. Every Starbucks was hiring, every drugstore and grocery. Have the employees who used to work there died? I wondered. Where was everyone?

When a teenager arrived to my book-signing stand, my first query was no longer "When did you last see your parents naked? " but "Do you have a job? "

Nine times out of ten, before the kid could talk, his or her mother would take control. "Tyler is too busy with his schoolwork," or "Kayla just needs to be seventeen now." On some occasions the person would be genderqueer, and the mother would add, "Cedar is taking some time to figure themself out."

There was a Willow as too, and a Hickory. I assumed it was a thing now to name yourself after a tree.

One woman I met, a mother of three, informed me that none of her teenagers held jobs and weren't likely to anytime soon. "Why should they bust their buttocks for $17 an hour? "

"Um, because it's seventeen more than they'd receive just sitting at home doing nothing? "

"I grew up having to work and don't want to put my kids in that headspace," the mom responded.

Dear God, I thought. America, as I knew it, is finished. Isn't it normal for a teenager to have a bad job? It's how you acquire compassion. My three oldest children worked in cafeterias, and Amy was a grocery cashier. Tiffany and Paul worked in kitchens. We made $1.60 per hour and, dammit, we were delighted. That's how this country operated. If you wanted a bong at the age of sixteen, you had to put in the effort. Now I'm guessing your folks just bought it for you and probably gave you the pot as well.

Toward the end of my tour, the New York Times published an article about how many schools were implementing virtual Fridays. Parents were outraged because they would now have to locate sitters or remain at home themselves that day. "Well, I think it's much needed," stated everyone instructor I spoke with. Everyone was commenting, "Our jobs are really stressful." Being a claims adjuster, leading an IT unit, and marketing eye shadow: "It's tough work that takes a toll on me! "

Because it was so difficult to locate and retain employees, people who would have been fired two years ago for various reasons remained in their positions—for example, the desk clerk at my Richmond, Virginia, hotel. I came just after midnight and found the place unoccupied. No one was in the lobby. "Hello! "I called. "Is anyone here?" "

When no one answered, I stepped behind the check-in desk to try again. "Hello? "

I walked to the bell stand and back. I peeked into the eatery, which was secured with a louvered metal fence. A few minutes passed, and just as I was considering calling a cab and checking into another hotel, a woman appeared—midforties, slightly untidy, and angry. Her mouth was tiny and resembled a recently healed exit wound. "What are you doing?" "She demanded. "You're not supposed to step behind my counter, especially during COVID. We cannot have anybody back here! "

"I'm sorry," I replied. "There was no one around, and I wasn't sure—"

"We know you're here," the woman said abruptly. "We have cameras. "We can see you."

I assumed I had never worked in a hotel. How am I expected to know about your setup? "If you saw me, why did you not come out? "I asked.

"I was busy," she explained. "Is it okay with you, me doing things? "

She had evidently been lying down. The only question was whether she had been alone or with someone. This was not a flophouse that rented rooms by the hour. My one-night stay was close to $200, but even if it were a tenth of that, you can't talk to your visitors like that, especially if they're courteous.

I had resolved that on my way out the next morning, I would tell on this woman, but when her associate inquired, "How was your stay?" I simply said, "Fine," thinking, as I often do when someone is nasty to me, that at least I can write about it.

Then I felt fortunate, not just to be back at work, but also to have the one job in America that wasn't too difficult to handle. Every night, as I walked from the stage wings to the podium, trying not to trip over my floor-length shirt, I'd think, "There is literally nothing to this." It had a heavy, braided hem, and I was distraught to discover one afternoon that I had left it in the closet of the motel I had checked out of earlier that morning. Of course, I contacted in the hopes of getting it back, but in retrospect, I should have answered, "Yes, I'm afraid my wife forgot to pack her nightgown." As it was, the desk clerk insisted that what had been turned in was most surely intended for a woman.

"Look at the tag," I instructed him. "It says Homme Plus." Homme means "man" in French.

The individual responded, "Yes, but this is...decorative."

On top of the numerous HELP WANTED banners and Christian T-shirts I observed people wearing—including ON MY BLESSED BEHAVIOR and LONG STORY SHORT: GOD SAVED MY LIFE—I realized how different it was to travel from one state to the next, or even from city to city within a single state. In Los Angeles, masks were required in all public areas of my hotel, and I had to provide proof of vaccination to access the restaurant. If I left for whatever reason, I'd have to display it again when I returned, because this was Los Angeles, where, unless you're famous or horrifically damaged, no one recalls your face—especially the top half of it—for more than five seconds, or three if you're over fifty. From there, I traveled to Palm Springs, where, aside from the workers dressed in black N95s, my hotel was completely open. It's worth noting that both of those hotels were upscale—a Four Seasons and a Ritz-Carlton.

From California, I flew to Montana. I donned a mask into my hotel lobby out of habit, and I received the same reactions as if I had worn an HILLARY CLINTON T-shirt to a Klan rally. The next afternoon, I went to lunch and was surprised to see that none of the personnel had their faces covered: not the hostess or the server, and neither of the cooks I could see when the kitchen door opened. For much of America—particularly the red parts—the pandemic had ended, at least on the ground, and wearing a mask made me feel uneasy.

Meanwhile, in the air, federal law required face covers. The pilots made regular announcements, but the flight attendants did much of the heavy work. Sometimes it was a lost battle. On an early-morning flight from Odessa, Texas, to Houston, several of my fellow passengers politely but firmly stated, "Nope." "I'm done with your regulations." Our flight attendant was only twenty-three years old, so what could she do? When she tried to scold the person next to me, he made a joke about her beauty.

"Sir, could you please cover your nose and mouth?" "

"You have a smokin' body."

"I beg your pardon?" "

"Nice face, too. "I want to see more of it."

It wasn't even nine a.m. yet, and he had already put away two double vodkas. "I'm going to slip that little girl a hundred dollars on my way off the plane," he said, his voice like tires on gravel, as we landed. "See if I don't, because that amount of money is nothing to me."

The man was right up in my face, his spittle flecking my spectacles, and I thought, "Really?" I'm going to obtain my COVID from you. Why couldn't it be from someone I like?

But I did not get sick. This is noteworthy because I was quite irresponsible. Most evenings, I removed my mask for book signings and pushed aside the plexiglass shield that should have been between me and the person I was speaking with. Otherwise, it was difficult to speak or listen. I rode in packed elevators and in cars with drivers whose lips, like mine, were rarely completely covered. Some establishments strictly enforced the mask policy, which was OK unless they were enforcing it on me. I preferred a situation in which I took no measures while the rest of the world was forced to double up. I preferred to be in a red state, maskless, and whining about how backward everyone around me was.

Tours have always been effective at bringing me out of my comfort zone, and this one was especially so. Driving across the Midwest, I saw one TRUMP 2024 sign after another—and the election was still three years away. "You know you're in a place that's inhospitable to liberals when you see fireworks stores," Adam commented in rural Indiana as we passed one powder keg after another.

"Fireworks are guns for children," I observed.

"They're the gateway drug," Adam acknowledged.

Then there were the actual guns—like the one I saw in Dayton, Ohio, while waiting in line for a cup of coffee. Ahead of me stood a group of three people, none of whom appeared to have ever been to Starbucks. Everyone had beards and wore no masks. Their features looked like those on a WANTED DEAD OR ALIVE poster from the Old West, but they were colorized. "What's the closest you came to a milkshake? " The tallest among them inquired of the peculiar small creature behind the counter. "Is the ice in a Mocha Cookie Crumble Frappuccino shaved or chunky?" "

A month ago, in a coffee shop in Springfield, Missouri, I noticed a sign for an Almond Joy Latte. Despite all of our discourse about health and, worse, "wellness," most Americans' burning question is, "How can we make this more fattening? "This has long been the case. I just noticed it because of my recent diet and struggle to maintain my weight loss. In Des Moines, I heard about a restaurant that served hamburgers on buns made of compressed macaroni cheese. When I saw "Vegan Soup" on a menu in Boston, my first thought was that it was made with the heaviest vegan they could find and boil, rather than that it had no butter or cream.

The three people in front of me at the Dayton Starbucks all ordered beverages with the mixer and massive amounts of whipped cream. The tallest of them then asked Donna if she wanted anything. She was out of the automobile, possibly bound and gagged in the trunk. As he reached into his back pocket for his phone, his shirt raised, and I noticed he had a pistol tucked inside his jeans. A school shooting had occurred twenty minutes earlier in Oxford Township, Michigan, so the image alarmed me more than it would have a day before. Are he and his companions planning to loot this place? I wondered. Or perhaps they had held up a gas station earlier in the afternoon and were now off duty. I mean, burglars don't rob every establishment they enter, right?

The America I saw in the fall of 2021 was tired and battle-hardened. The walkways were cracked. Its mailboxes were smashed in. I saw tent cities all across the West Coast. They were in parks, abandoned lots, and crumbling squares. In one trip after another, I'd arrive at a store or restaurant I recalled only to find it boarded up or perhaps burned out, the plywood blocking the doors covered in graffiti: EAT THE RICH. FUCK THE POLICE. BLACK LIVES MATTERS.

During my year and a half back home, I had forgotten the ups and downs of life on tour. One night you're at Symphony Hall, the next you're in a dilapidated, once-grand movie theater infested with mice. "Could you believe they intended to demolish this place? " the home manager always asks, joyfully staring up at a gold plaster cherub with one arm missing.

"Um, yes, as a matter of fact."

It's the same for hotels. I traveled from the new Four Seasons in Philadelphia to the Four Points by Sheraton on the side of an eight-lane road in York, Pennsylvania. It was a Friday, and all of the guests had tattoos on their necks except for me and a very angry mother of the bride, who had two smudged butterflies above her right ankle. My room was at the back of the building, and whenever I looked out the window, I noticed people gathered in the parking lot. Is there a fire drill that I missed? I would wonder.

The next morning, I went out back to see what all the fuss was about and discovered a pile of human feces next to a face mask that someone had wiped their ass on.

It was off to the Ritz-Carlton in Washington, DC at noon, and the next day, at breakfast in the ground-floor restaurant, I saw a woman at the table next to me request an extra plate. She loaded it with bacon and eggs and laid it on the carpet for her tiny terrier to eat from.

Honestly? I thought. On the carpet? After finishing his breakfast, the dog strayed. People's routes were impeded by his extendable leash, but no one seemed to notice except me, who had remained seated and thus was not inconvenienced. "Oh my God! "My fellow guests cried, as if they had accidentally across a baby panda. "How adorable are you?" " One woman revealed that she had two fur puppies waiting for her at home.

"It must kill you to be separated from them," the whore who had placed the plate on the carpet murmured.

"Oh, it does," confessed the jism-soaked hag who had initiated the talk. "But they'll see Mommy soon enough."

Was feeding your dog from a plate in the dining room preferable than wiping your ass with a face mask? Difficult to say, really. Both were pretty hard to take. That said, if you're after a decent night's sleep, your safest bet is the Ritz, where most of the guests have at least stayed in a hotel before and know better than to yell, "Bro, you are so fucking high right now! " outside your door at three a.m.

Whenever the extremes got to me, I'd comfort myself with the many interesting people I met as I made my way across the country—a woman, for instance, whose father had executed her pet hamster with a .22 rifle.

"But why?" I asked.

"Butterscotch had a virus that caused all her hair to fall out," she told me.

Then there was the psychologist whose father's last words to her, croaked out on his deathbed, were "You are a communist cunt."

The most haunting person was someone I had never met in person. In the middle of my tour, I was scheduled to fly from Springfield, Missouri, to Chicago for a night off. I arrived at the airport early, checked my bag, and was walking outside to get some steps in when I received notification that my flight—and all planes to Chicago—had been canceled. So I asked whether a car could be arranged. One was, and while I waited for it to arrive, I took some more steps. I couldn't travel far because I needed to keep an eye on my luggage, so I wandered around the baggage carousels, which were all empty. As I passed one of them, I noticed two pairs of filthy underwear huddled in its gutter, an almost empty Tic Tac dispenser, a brush with strands of long, strawberry-blond hair tangled in it, three AA batteries, and a small sheaf of toothpicks. It was such an interesting portrayal of someone—a young woman, I assumed—and I thought of her for months to come, wondering, as I moved from place to place in this divided, beat-up country of ours, where she was and what she imagined had become of her underwear.

The contents of this book may not be copied, reproduced or transmitted without the express written permission of the author or publisher. Under no circumstances will the publisher or author be responsible or liable for any damages, compensation or monetary loss arising from the information contained in this book, whether directly or indirectly. .

Disclaimer Notice:

Although the author and publisher have made every effort to ensure the accuracy and completeness of the content, they do not, however, make any representations or warranties as to the accuracy, completeness, or reliability of the content. , suitability or availability of the information, products, services or related graphics contained in the book for any purpose. Readers are solely responsible for their use of the information contained in this book

Every effort has been made to make this book possible. If any omission or error has occurred unintentionally, the author and publisher will be happy to acknowledge it in upcoming versions.

Copyright © 2025

All rights reserved.

Printed in Dunstable, United Kingdom